BELONGING

*Bonds of Healing
and Recovery*

also from the authors
published by Paulist Press

DELIVERANCE PRAYER
HEALING LIFE'S HURTS
HEALING OF MEMORIES
HEALING THE DYING (with Mary Jane Linn, C.S.J.)
HEALING THE EIGHT STAGES OF LIFE
HEALING THE GREATEST HURT
PRAYER COURSE FOR HEALING LIFE'S HURTS
PRAYING WITH ANOTHER FOR HEALING

BELONGING

Bonds of Healing and Recovery

Dennis Linn
Sheila Fabricant Linn
Matthew Linn, S.J.

PAULIST PRESS
New York/Mahwah, N.J.

Photo Credits:
Cover, Richard Strauss; p. 6, Wilson House; p. 18, Steve and Mary Skjold Photographs; p. 36, L & C Tidd; p. 54, Gene Plaisted; p. 84, Orville Andrews; p. 106, Kay Freeman; p. 118, Cleo Freelance Photo; p. 148, Vernon Sigl; p. 166, Mia et Klaus; p. 194, White Eyes Design

IMPRIMI POTEST:
Bert R. Thelen, S.J.
Provincial, Wisconsin Province
November 12, 1991

Library of Congress Cataloging-in-Publication Data

Linn, Dennis.
    Belonging : bonds of healing and recovery / Dennis Linn, Sheila Fabricant Linn, Matthew Linn.
       p.   cm.
    ISBN 0-8091-3365-2
    1. Co-dependence (Psychology)—Religious aspects—Christianity.
2. Twelve-step programs—Religious aspects—Christianity—
Meditations.   3. Pastoral counseling.   I. Linn, Sheila Fabricant.
II. Linn, Matthew.   III. Title.
BV4596.C57L56   1993
248.8'6—dc20   92-29855
                                 CIP

Published by Paulist Press
977 Macarthur Boulevard
Mahwah, N.J. 07430

Printed and bound in the United States of America

Contents

This book
is gratefully dedicated to

Jack (The King) McGinnis

who stands by his friends.

ACKNOWLEDGMENTS

We wish to thank those who gave us the gift of their time and loving care in reading the manuscript for this book and offering helpful suggestions: Dr. Daniel J. Anderson, Maria Esther Castillo, M.A., Dr. Kathleen Fischer, Robert Flanagan, Virginia Flanagan, Rev. Edmund Griesedieck, Dr. Morton Kelsey, Marion Mann, R.N., Elia Maqueo, Tesha Martinez-Baez, Rev. Jack McGinnis, Dr. Arnold W. Mech, Dr. Susan Delaney Mech, Pat & Pia Mellody, Dr. Douglas Schoeninger, Rev. Robert Sears, S.J. and Dr. Diana Villegas. Thanks also to Dennis and Matt's parents, Leonard and Agnes May Linn, for proofreading, encouragement and good food.

The publisher gratefully acknowledges use of excerpts from the following sources: *Twelve Steps and Twelve Traditions* (Alcoholics Anonymous World Services [hereafter AAWS], 1953); *As Bill Sees It* (AAWS, 1967); *Alcoholics Anonymous* (AAWS, 1976);*Alcoholics Anonymous Comes of Age* by William Wilson (AAWS, 1979); *Pass It On* (AAWS, 1984). The foregoing materials are reprinted with permission of Alcoholics Anonymous World Services, Inc. Permission to reprint this material does not mean that AA has reviewed or approved the contents of this publication, nor that AA agrees with the views expressed herein. AA is a program of recovery from alcoholism *only*. *Bill W.* by Robert Thomsen. Copyright © 1975 by Robert Thomsen. Reprinted by permission of International Creative Management, Inc. and HarperCollins Publishers. *Addiction and Grace* by Gerald May. Copyright © 1988 by Gerald May. Reprinted by permission of HarperCollins Publishers. *Facing Codependence* by Pia Mellody with Andrea Wells Miller and Keith Miller. Copyright © 1989 by Pia Mellody Enterprises and J. Keith Miller and Andrea Wells Miller. Reprinted by permission of HarperCollins Publishers. *Not-God: A History of Alcoholics Anonymous* by Ernest Kurtz, copyright 1991, Hazelden Foundation, Center City, MN. Reprinted by permission. *Don't Call It Love: Recovery from Sexual Addiction* by Patrick J. Carnes, Ph.D. Copyright © 1991 by Patrick J. Carnes, Ph.D. Used by permission of Bantam Books, a division of Bantam Doubleday Dell Publishing Group, Inc. *The Recovery Resource Book* by Barbara Yoder. Copyright © 1990 by Wink Books. Reprinted by permission of Simon and Schuster. *Banished Knowledge* by Alice Miller, copyright 1990. Used by permission of Doubleday, a division of Bantam Doubleday Dell Publishing Group, Inc. *Redemptive Intimacy: A New Perspective for the Journey to Adult Faith*, copyright 1981, Twenty-Third Publications, Mystic, CT, paper, 176 pp., $5.95. Used by permission.

Preface

Last year we visited the Wilson House in Vermont, the old inn where Bill Wilson (co-founder of Alcoholics Anonymous) was born. The inn has been restored and is now a center for A.A. and Al-Anon recovery. We overheard the following conversation between two other guests, a young woman named Susan and an A.A. oldtimer named Joe, on their way out of an A.A. meeting:

Susan: I've been getting to know my inner child lately, and my therapist is encouraging me to get in touch with my anger.

Joe: Just keep workin' them 12 Steps, honey.

Susan: My boundaries aren't very good, and I want to get better at saying "No."

Joe: Just keep workin' them Steps, honey.

Susan: My spiritual director is helping me learn to trust that my higher power isn't like my parents, who abused me. I wonder if I'll ever get well.

Joe: (with immense love in his voice) I know where you're at, honey. I've been there too. Them Steps worked for me. I support ya.

In this book, we want to integrate Susan's psychological and spiritual insight with Joe's simple, loving wisdom, as is happening throughout the 12 Step movement. Although we are used to speaking Susan's language, we find we have a lot in common with Joe's A.A. world and the 12 Step recovery movement which has emerged from it.

Our roots in Ignatian spirituality have helped us integrate Joe's and Susan's worlds. These roots have given us a basically optimistic view of creation and have taught us to trust experience. We instinctively look for the presence of God in all things, and this incarnational attitude is at the core of the 12 Step movement as well. From the beginning, A.A. relied not upon doctrines or absolutes to attract members, but upon the power of shared experience and a commitment to telling the truth about what *is*.[1] The basis of discernment in 12 Step groups is group conscience, which simply means that group members get in touch with their life experience and trust that God will speak through it. Joe keeps returning to the 12 Steps because he knows from experience that "Them Steps work." This same process of reflection upon experience is the basis of Ignatian discernment. Moreover, the goal of Ignatian spirituality is "indifference," meaning freedom to choose the greatest good without being swayed by compulsive attachments. What better description of recovery from addictions? Perhaps the parallels between 12 Step recovery and Ignatian spirituality should not surprise us, since Bill Wilson's spiritual mentor was the Jesuit priest, Ed Dowling.

Our work has always been to integrate spirituality with psychology, a natural movement for us since our incarnational attitude has led us to trust what we can learn from science. We all have training in pastoral psychology, which has taught us to see childhood hurts as fundamental to problems in later life. We have also learned to trust emotions and the developmental process, and to see the self as a composite of many parts seeking integration.

Finally, we have worked extensively with healing prayer in the context of Catholic Charismatic Renewal. Healing prayer taught us that Jesus is a real and present person who can heal our emotional wounds. See, for example, Sheila's story of healing sexual abuse through healing prayer in Chapter Seven and Matt's experience of healing anger in Chapters Four and Seven.

We think Bill Wilson would understand our effort to integrate psychology, spirituality and 12 Step recovery. He wrote,

> We welcome new and valuable knowledge whether it issues from a test tube, from a psychiatrist's couch, or from revealing social studies . . . we can accomplish together what we could never accomplish in separation and rivalry.[2]

The genius of 12 Step recovery is in sharing experience by sharing our stories. We'll begin by sharing Bill W.'s story, and in the rest of this book we will share our own stories. Since we are Christians and some of our healing has come through inner healing prayer, we will be sharing our experience of Jesus' healing love. We do this because it is the most authentic way we can speak of God as we understand God. The 12 Steps, however, welcome each person to relate to God as *he or she* understands God. Bill W. knew that healthy religious faith can grow only in an atmosphere of freedom, not coercion. Moreover, he never forgot what Ed Dowling told him during their first meeting: "If you can name it, it's not God."[3] What mattered most to Bill was that people got well, and he trusted that their experience of recovery would lead them to God in their own way and in their own time:

> . . . we question very much whether our Buddhist members in Japan would ever have joined this Society had A.A. officially stamped itself a strictly Christian movement.
> You can easily convince yourself of this by imagining that A.A. started among the Buddhists and that they then told you you couldn't join them unless you became a Buddhist, too. If you were a Christian alcoholic under these circumstances, you might as well turn your face to the wall and die.[4]

Therefore, we don't want to impose our experience upon you. Instead, we hope that we can share our experience of God in a way that puts you in touch with yours, however different that may be.

After Bill W.'s story and two of our own, Chapter Four and the following chapters in this book take the 12 Steps in order. This format is not meant as a blueprint, but rather as a suggested way to get in touch with where you are and be loved in it. Perhaps you will want to set aside a particular Step and go on to a later one or go back to an earlier one, much as happens in 12 Step groups where members are free to work on whatever Step they need most. In 1934 Bill W. went right from Steps 1, 2, and 3 to Step 12, and not until 1940 did he thoroughly do Steps 4 and 5 with Ed Dowling.

The special gift of 12 Step recovery is that whatever the order in which we work the Steps, we may work them with the help of others. Thus, perhaps you will wish to share this book with a friend. Perhaps you will feel drawn to do this in a 12 Step group where you can receive the healing love of a community and sponsor. Perhaps you belong to another group where you feel safe to share yourself, e.g., your family, therapy group, church fellowship, study group, etc. If you want to share what you experience here in a structured way with any of these groups, Appendix B is a course guide for using this book (and accompanying tapes, if you wish) as a course for two or more people.

CHAPTER ONE

Bill W. and the Search for Belonging

The movie "E.T." is about a person from another planet who wants to go home to where he belongs. E.T. accidentally gets left on earth when his people come here in a spaceship to explore. Separated from them, he begins to die. E.T. knows where he belongs and he tries to reach his people. He figures out a way to phone home by making a radio from spare parts in the garage of the house where he is hiding out from earth scientists and police. No one comes. E.T.'s body shrivels up and his heart stops beating. The scientists who finally find his hiding place think he's dead. They are ready to take his body away to cut it up and study it. Then suddenly his heart starts beating again, all because E.T. knows his people are coming for him.

"E.T." has sold more copies on videotape than any other movie ever made. Perhaps this movie is so popular because we identify with E.T.'s longing to go home to where he belongs. Somewhere deep inside each of us remembers where we came from. We keep sending out signals, trying to phone home and hoping someone will answer us. Our very addictions can be the best way we know at the time to phone home. Bill Wilson, co-founder of Alcoholics Anonymous, knew that belonging was the key to recovery and healing. So, in this chapter I (Sheila) want to begin with Bill W.'s story.

Bill W.'s Story

Bill W. was born in 1895 in Vermont and he died in 1971. His mother was a rather cold and distant person. Bill felt closer to his father, a warm, loving man who came from an alcoholic family and drank a lot himself. One evening in 1905 when Bill was nine, his father took him out for a long ride to the marble quarry in the Green Mountains that overlooked their home. Along the way Bill's father kept drinking from a jug of whiskey. That evening, Bill

> felt closer to his father than he'd ever felt to anyone; he felt a part of him. . . . It came to him that he didn't only feel a part of his father, he *was* a part of him—just as he was part of his grandfather and he in turn of his father. . . . Billy watched him with a sense of awe, aware of something—he had no other word for it—of something *ancestral* in himself.
>
> And Billy listened to everything his father said about the night, the heavens, the vast galaxies sailing through space. His father could locate and identify each constellation, each star and planet . . . he told Billy that they weren't just citizens of Vermont or even just the United States; they were citizens of this whole tremendous universe.[1]

All the while, and all during the long ride home that followed, Bill's father kept drinking from the jug. Thus, early in his life, Bill's memories of belonging to his father, his ancestors, and "this whole tremendous universe" became connected with a jug of whiskey.

The next morning when Bill woke up, his sister told him that their father had left. Bill never saw his father again until 1914, nine years later, and by then the closeness between them was gone. It seems to us that Bill spent the rest of his life searching for the sense of belonging he felt that evening with his father when he was nine—belonging to himself, to his ancestors, to the universe and to the God who made it all.

Soon after Bill's father left, his mother got a divorce. Like many children of divorce, Bill blamed himself:

> If only his parents had loved him more, they wouldn't have separated. And this meant if he had been more lovable, it never would have happened. It always came around to that. It was, it *had to be* his fault. He was the guilty one.[2]

Bill spoke of the stigma and disgrace associated with divorce in 1905, and how it led him to feel "that I didn't belong, I was somehow different."[3] Bill's mother decided to study in Boston. She left Bill with her parents. Although he lost both his parents within a short time, Bill never grieved his loss. He even bragged that he didn't grieve and went on with life "like a man."

Bill's losses did not end with his parents. In high school, he and Bertha, a classmate, fell in love. For the first time since his father left, Bill felt that he belonged to someone: "I had romance, security and applause. I was ecstatically happy." Then, Bertha died suddenly. Bill fell into a profound depression that lasted three years, and did not graduate with his class. Bill recalled, "I was unable to finish because I could not accept the loss of any part of what I thought *belonged* to me."[4] [italics ours]

At age twenty-two while attending a party, Bill felt inferior, awkward and socially inept, as he often did. Then someone offered him his first drink. Years later, Bill wrote,

> My self-consciousness was such that I simply had to take that drink. So, I took it, and another one, and then. . . . That strange barrier that existed between me and all men and women seemed to instantly go down. *I felt that I belonged where I was, belonged to life; I belonged to the universe; I was a part of things at last.* Oh, the magic of those first three or four

> drinks! I became the life of the party. . . . I think, even that
> first evening, I got thoroughly drunk, and within the next time
> or two I passed out completely. But as everybody drank hard,
> nothing too much was made of that.[5] [italics ours]

Bill's first drink gave him what he knew he most needed at the time to survive: a sense of belonging. From then on he became progressively addicted to alcohol.

In 1918 Bill married Lois Burnham. They moved to New York City where Bill became a stockbroker. He was the first person on Wall Street to figure out how to study a business and determine whether it would succeed. Bill was very successful initially. However, as his gift for business was developing, so was his alcoholism. Several employers fired Bill for drinking. Eventually his reputation on Wall Street was that of a drunk and no one would hire him.

After each drinking binge he promised Lois that now he would stay sober. It never lasted. He was hospitalized for alcoholism several times. Finally his doctor told Bill that alcohol had so damaged his mind and body that he probably would go crazy and die.

Bill's friend, Ebby, was also an alcoholic. Ebby had been attending meetings of the Oxford Group, a religious revival that was very popular in the 1930's. When Ebby visited him in the hospital, Bill could see that Ebby had changed. Ebby told Bill that God had helped him to stop drinking. Bill found that hard to believe. He wasn't sure there was a God, and if there was he wasn't sure that God could help *him*. Finally Bill was so desperate that one night in the hospital he cried out to the God he didn't believe in. He describes what happened next:

> Suddenly my room blazed with an indescribable white light.
> I was seized with an ecstasy beyond description. . . . Then,
> seen in the mind's eye, there was a mountain. I stood upon

its summit, where a great wind blew. A wind, not of air, but of spirit. In great, clean strength, it blew right through me. Then came the blazing thought, "You are a free man." . . . a great peace stole over me. . . . I became acutely conscious of a Presence which seemed like a veritable sea of living spirit. . . . "This," I thought, "must be the great reality. The God of the preachers." I seemed to be possessed by the absolute, and the curious conviction deepened that no matter how wrong things seemed to be, there could be no question of the ultimate rightness of God's universe. *For the first time I felt that I really belonged.* I knew that I was loved and could love in return.[6] [italics ours]

Bill never took another drink. It was 1934 and he was 39 years old.

The accounts of Bill's conversion and his first drink are very similar.[7] Bill even uses the same words to describe both experiences: "*I felt that I belonged.*" Perhaps Bill began the 12-Step movement to give to others the same sense of belonging that he searched for all his life and that freed him from alcoholism:

. . . "salvation" in Alcoholics Anonymous consisted in "emerging from isolation" to the "feeling of being at one with God and man," to "the sense of *belonging* that comes to us. We no longer live in a completely hostile world. We are no longer lost and frightened and purposeless."[8] [italics Bill Wilson's]

Immediately after his conversion experience, Bill, with Lois, began trying to help other alcoholics. He had little success at first. His focus was on how *they* needed his help, but somehow *they* didn't seem to appreciate it. A few months later he went to Akron, Ohio on business. It was a stressful trip, compounded by the pressure he felt to recover his reputation as a reliable stockbroker. Staying in a hotel by himself, Bill felt very lonely. There was a bar at one end of the lobby and he felt tempted to walk over and get a drink. Then the thought came to him, "*You* need another alcoholic to talk to; *you* need another alcoholic just as much as he needs you."[9]

Instead of walking over to the bar, he walked over to the other end of the lobby where there was a telephone and a directory of local churches. He called church pastors until he found one who could lead him to an alcoholic, "Dr. Bob" Smith. Instead of Bill getting drunk that weekend, he and Dr. Bob met for what would become known as the first A.A. meeting. As Bill described it, "In the kinship of common suffering, one alcoholic had been talking to another."[10]

Just by sharing their stories with each other, Bill and Dr. Bob discovered the key to the whole 12 Step movement: two people sharing the same struggle can give one another the sense of belonging that helps them both to get well. At a time when the recovery rate through other methods was about zero, Bill and Dr. Bob knew that what helped them could help other alcoholics. During the next two years, they helped forty alcoholics to recover.

The Growth of the 12 Step Movement

Bill had earned a reputation on Wall Street as a genius by analyzing what works in business. Now he used that same genius to identify what works in helping an alcoholic to recover. He wrote down a list of twelve principles that worked. These became the Twelve Steps. The Steps drew on Bill's experience of himself and other alcoholics, on what he learned from the Oxford Group and on his reading of the Bible.

The A.A. movement grew quickly after publication of Bill's book, *Alcoholics Anonymous* ("The Big Book"). Today hundreds of thousands of groups in almost every country in the world, and millions of alcoholics identify themselves as part of A.A. In New York City alone, as of 1988 there were 1800 different A.A. meetings each week.[11] We have visited tiny villages in the mountains of Guatemala and seen signs for the meeting places of "Alcoholicos Anonimos." A.A.'s success has been documented. For example, the Rand Study found that of those who attend meetings regularly for one year, 70% remain sober for a second year, and of those 90% have a third year of sobriety.[12]

In 1950, Lois Wilson founded Al-Anon as a support group for the family members of an alcoholic. Lois realized that they needed the same 12 Steps that helped the alcoholic. Al-Anon then contributed to the discovery of codependency. Like Lois, therapists who worked with addicts noticed that when an addict began to get well, family members sometimes became very upset. It appeared that people close to an addict tended to get their identity from taking care of the addict. Such people were dependent on the person who was dependent on alcohol or drugs or whatever; they were codependent. Thus, people who grew up in an alcoholic family learned as children to orient themselves around the needs of an alcoholic mother or father. As adults they tended to marry someone whom they could continue to take care of, e.g., another alcoholic. It became evident that these people needed a process of recovery as much as the addict. Our understanding of codependency has since broadened to include people from any type of dysfunctional family in which they learned to deny their own needs, whether or not they have ever lived with a chemically dependent person. Today the fastest growing 12 Step groups are Codependents Anonymous (Coda) and Adult Children of Alcoholics (ACOA).[13]

Since 1950, application of the 12 Steps has grown immensely. We've learned that people who overwork, gamble uncontrollably, compulsively overeat or act out sexually aren't just people with bad habits who lack "will-power." They are addicts, too. They can't stop any more than an alcoholic can stop. They can be helped by the same 12 Step program that helps alcoholics. While the physical predisposition and social conditioning for one or another addiction might be different, similar psychological dynamics underlie any addictive behavior. For example, I come from a Jewish family with no history of alcoholism. When I'm in a compulsive state, I am not tempted to drink. Like my family of origin, my temptations are worry and overwork. If I had a physical predisposition to alcoholism and/or if I had grown up with alcoholics, perhaps I would drink instead.

Physical predisposition and social conditioning affect which addiction we choose. But whether we worry, overwork, drink, overeat, etc., whenever we're involved in addictive behavior, the psychological dynamics are similar. Twelve Step groups like Gamblers' Anonymous, Overeaters Anonymous, Sex & Love Addicts Anonymous, etc. work with these similar psychological dynamics. Today there are over 200 *different* groups based on the 12 Steps and more than fifteen million Americans attend a weekly support group meeting.[14]

Addictions, Connectedness and Belonging

Pia Mellody, an internationally known expert on recovery, believes that underlying every addiction is codependency, the ignoring of one's own needs. She sees codependency as rooted in abuse (sexual, physical, emotional, intellectual, spiritual), broadly defined as "any experience in childhood (birth to age seventeen) that is less than nurturing."[15] Dr. Patrick Carnes, a foremost authority on sexual addiction, agrees: "Our research demonstrates that child abuse is an essential cause of addiction . . . the more abused you are as a child, the more addictions you are likely to have as an adult."[16] When our human needs for nurture are frustrated through abuse, we use addictions to fill our emptiness. Gershen Kaufman writes,

> The alcoholic who has a relationship with his bottle has substituted something else for a human relationship. The

addiction is the substitute for interpersonal needs. There has been a critical failure in the human environment and a sense of shame surrounds those vital inter-personal needs we all experience.[17]

In Bill W.'s own words, "defective relations with other human beings have nearly always been the immediate cause of our woes, including our alcoholism . . ."[18]

We believe all addictions and all recovery from addictions come from the deep longing we share with Bill Wilson, to *feel that I belong.* Jack McGinnis, who does some of the best 12 Step work we know, speaks of this in terms of our search for "connectedness" where we feel "disconnectedness."[19] We all came into existence with a consciousness, a felt sense, that we were connected to the sources of life out of which we came. We felt connected to God, to the significant people who received us in this world, to the universe and to our true self. Psalm 139 is about this sense of primal connectedness: "before you formed me in the womb you knew me."

Some of us, especially if we suffered early emotional deprivation, may be out of touch with these primal memories, but we all have the *capacity* to remember where we came from and how connected we were.[20] Many people have shared with us memories of the womb and of their conception.[21] Some can remember back through the evolutionary process to the formation of our planet or the first appearance of living organisms. Even if they have no training in botany or biology they can describe the life processes going on with an accuracy that seems impossible if they were not really remembering something.[22] Scientists know now that memory is found not only in the brain. The protein in each cell contains a form of memory.[23] Our cells remember where we came from and that we were created connected to all life.

When we are born into this world, if the people around us cannot protect and nurture our sense of connectedness to all life, we suffer hurts. If we have no way to work through our feelings about those hurts, we get disconnected from our true selves. When we are disconnected from ourselves, we cannot connect authentically with others, God or the universe. Like E.T., we begin searching for some way to reconnect. Addictions are our best attempt at the time to reconnect, although ultimately they don't work and become destructive. When Bill Wilson took his first drink, he felt reconnected. He felt that he belonged. But alcohol was a false connection. Bill stopped drinking only when he found a real connection through his conversion experience of a loving God.

We (and Bill) Are Still Learning

Bill's conversion experience gave him enough real sense of belonging that he stopped drinking. However, he was not completely healed. For eleven years after he stopped drinking, he suffered from depression. He was a workaholic and we ourselves were surprised to read of evidence that Bill may have been a sex addict. Many people in A.A. knew that Bill had a series of mistresses, and in his will he left part of his book royalties to his last one.[24] After chain-smoking all his life, Bill finally died of emphysema.

We can only guess what Bill needed to help him with these other addictions. For example, when we learn about the alcoholism in Bill's family, how he never grieved the loss of his parents, and the devastating loss of his girlfriend, we wonder if an ACOA group would have helped him. Perhaps there he could have worked through some of his early hurts.[25] Or, when we consider how, as A.A. grew, the needs of the movement consumed Bill, we wish he had understood codependency and how to care for his own needs as a balance to caring for others.[26]

We can only guess, and we don't blame Bill for the problems in his life that remained unresolved. Only since he died, have we learned the importance of grieving our losses, especially major ones such as the loss of parents. We're only beginning to understand what happens to children in alcoholic families and about codependency. We're learning these things partly because we're building on what Bill discovered about recovery from alcoholism. Bill himself said that there was more to be learned. He saw the 12 Steps as only a beginning, and he exhorted A.A. to continue learning from new experiences.[27] For Bill, surrender to a higher power included surrendering any claim to having the final answer—even in the treatment of alcoholics.[28]

I like to think that Bill is helping us learn more. Recovery is a process that continues throughout this life and into the next. I believe that those who have gone on to the next life send back to us all the new things they are learning as they are healed. As a Roman Catholic, I interpret this in terms of the communion of saints.[29] Others, who come from different traditions, may interpret the same reality in a different way. Although we can only imagine how Bill is learning and growing in the next world, it does seem significant to us that so many new discoveries about addictions, codependency and the importance of grieving childhood losses have come to us since Bill's death in 1971. The last time we visited Bill's birthplace in East Dorsett, Vermont, I sat in the room where he was born, looking at his picture. I asked him to intercede for us as we write this book. It seemed to me that he promised he would, and that he wanted to thank us for being his friends. I think Bill has many friends, some of whom are teaching the three of us, and that he is interceding for us all.

CHAPTER TWO

Two of Our Stories

THE TWELVE STEPS ARE FOR EVERYONE

As a culture, we are growing more disconnected from God, nature, others and our deeper self. Each day one more endangered species of plant or animal life disappears. We destroy our rain forests to live in concrete canyons where our feet never touch the ground to root themselves in bare earth. Our families are rootless too, with the average family moving every three years. Yet sociologists say it takes three years to build a support network of friends. [1] In the U.S. two out of every three first marriages end in divorce with the average marriage lasting only seven years. [2] Because of this, 60% of the children who reach adolescence in the year 2000 will neither be living with nor supported by their birth fathers. [3] Every year more mothers must work to support the family and have less time to bond with children.

At the same time that the cultural sources of bonding and belonging are breaking down, the 12 Step movement is growing rapidly. For millions this movement is the primary way they fulfill their need to belong. [4] So, on the one hand, it feels strange to be writing a book on A.A.'s 12 Steps because I (Matt) have no substance addictions and did not grow up in an alcoholic home. Yet, as Bill W. states on the first page of *Twelve Steps and Twelve Traditions*, the 12 Steps have proved "a way to happy and effective living" not just for alcoholics but for everyone longing to

belong in a healing community. Perhaps that will be clearer if I
share my 12 Step journey.

Discovering My Need for the 12 Steps

My journey began in 1967 on the Rosebud Sioux Reservation when I took my alcoholic students to A.A. meetings. The
meetings were definitely anonymous for no one could see anyone
in the smoke filled rectory basement. I went to meetings for my
students' good, not mine. That changed a few years later when I
studied in Cambridge. The person most full of life in my Jesuit
community was seventy-year-old Philip who could hardly walk
but knew every alcoholic in Boston. Philip loved teaching but
with his advanced diabetes he could only stay home and give an
occasional reading course, such as his whimsically titled, "A Full
Explanation of the Mystery of God." To my surprise Philip felt no
bitterness over his handicap. He claimed that he was among the
first Jesuits in A.A. Philip felt most alive when on the phone
helping his pigeons (those he sponsored) stay sober. He had the
knack of knowing whom to call just as they were going out the
door to drink. He also had the knack of banging up our car when
going to nightly A.A. meetings, since he couldn't see well but
would never admit it. One of us always feigned interest in going
to A.A. in order to drive him. I wanted to find out what made
Philip loving and serene despite all his handicaps, so I gladly took
up chauffering him.

I found myself returning each week, even when he didn't
need a ride, because of what was happening to me at the meetings. It was the one place where I could be real, feel all my
feelings and after the meeting share with Philip my struggles. I
never shared much of myself during the meeting because I didn't
have a substance addiction and felt my conflicts with anger, etc.
were too petty. Yet as members shared their problems with anger

and what helped, I grew more in touch with my anger and what helped. I grew to appreciate A.A. even more as I listened to Fifth Step confessions that were the most honest and thorough confessions I ever heard. As I heard each confession I felt tremendous love for the other who had so many of my struggles. Each confession healed me by putting me in touch with both my struggles and God's healing love. That wasn't happening at the local prayer group that was long on praising God and praying for healing but short on sharing painful feelings. The prayer group brought healing not found at the A.A. meeting but the meeting brought honesty and self-knowledge not found at the prayer group. I needed both.

Three years later I returned to visit my Sioux friends after an absence of seven years. I kept asking "Who do you think has changed for the better since I left? What one person has changed the most? Why?" It was a great way to discover their role models and ideals on a reservation where 70% are alcoholic and growth is very difficult. I then listed those who grew moderately and those who everyone thought grew the most. To my surprise most of those in the moderate growth column all participated in a group where they felt they belonged and they could share their struggles and faith, e.g., A.A. or the reservation prayer group. Then I looked at the column of those who grew the most. I found that all but one participated in both A.A. and the prayer group. Something from each experience was helping them grow, just as it helped me.

Ten years later I again returned to the reservation and drew up the same lists with the same results. Only now these same people were even healthier. One had bounced back amazingly well from the loss of a child. Another, a school alcoholism counselor, could reach kids and adults no one else could help. I celebrated New Year's with these people, playing charades and drinking hot apple cider. I also made a New Year's resolution: I have to find a way to make the 12 Steps a bigger part of my life.

Since then I have participated in Adult Children of Alcoholics
and Codependents Anonymous meetings.

Dealing with My Addictions

But I am ahead of my story because I haven't shared how I
need help for my compulsive patterns. In 1985 I went to Bolivia
with Dennis and Sheila to learn Spanish. I had never studied
Spanish. I decided that the best way to learn was instant immer-
sion by living with a Bolivian family that knew no English. The
family was going through lots of stress since their father, Guti,
was dying of leukemia (he died in my fourth month with them). I
grew to love Guti who became like a father to me too. So I felt not
just the stress of learning Spanish in a foreign culture but also the
family's pain. All this took its toll and I needed time for grieving.
But the three of us were writing and presenting a talk in Spanish
each week at a conference center. That put extra pressure on me
because I had a harder time learning Spanish than Dennis or
Sheila. Thus instead of grieving, I became a workaholic in Spanish studies.

Henri Nouwen in *Gracias* writes of how learning Spanish at
this same school put him in touch with his primitive responses,
just as therapy did, because all the security of home and belonging is absent.[5] That happened to me. I became a chocoholic
needing to carry U.S. chocolate chips to eat whenever I was
studying. A struggle with sexual fantasies returned. I distracted
myself with compulsive shopping in the open market or English
TV and magazines. The language institute had a few English
movies on videotape. The sound was so garbled they could just as
well have been in Spanish. Still I was glued to movies such as
"Dracula" that in the U.S. I thought were a waste of time.

Little things bothered me, such as when someone grabbed
the new *Newsweek* and *Time* magazines before I could. I would

reread them several times a week. To my surprise I compre-
hended little of what I read because my inner pain was registering
more than the outside world. I couldn't forgive myself for making
the same Spanish mistakes repeatedly. I had a daily argument
with Dennis or Sheila over trivia such as which teacher was the
best or the worst. I needed to compare everything, improve it,
and be right.

I tried to change these patterns but couldn't. My anger
would find another target such as daily complaints about the
gloomy, rainy season. I went from thinking about chocolate to
thinking about the pizza I would enjoy after we finally presented
the week's Spanish talk. When I tried to do without something I
wanted or when I failed where I expected success, I became more
irritable and couldn't concentrate on my studies. I had physical
symptoms such as a tense stomach, headaches and tiredness. I
noticed these symptoms surfaced especially when I felt shame:
alienation from my true self because I was angry at myself and not
just at my mistakes.

Each evening Dennis, Sheila and I came together to share
what gave us life and what in the day drained life from us. This is
how I discovered that the above were becoming compulsive patterns. I also found what broke their compulsive power. I would be
more free and experience more peace on days when I could
accept my feelings. Just sharing in the evening both my times of
being loved and my struggles brought more peace. When I could
grieve how I was losing Guti and couldn't even lead the family in
the Spanish prayers they requested, I found deeper peace. I also
felt better when I could forgive myself for making more mistakes
than my Spanish partner or could ask forgiveness for being sharp
with another. My best prayer was to feel a struggle and then sit in
the sunny garden and with the plants soak up God's love for me.
Another day I felt more whole after playing with Guti's grandson
and holding him on my lap. I am sure that I was not just stroking
him but at some level also stroking my wounded inner child.

Whenever I felt that I belonged to myself, to others, to the universe, and to God with all my powerlessness, healing happened. I had experienced this at A.A. meetings, only now I was experiencing how it was freeing me and not just reserved for alcoholics.

Four years later when Dennis married Sheila, I grieved how we had been together for twenty-seven years of life in the same Jesuit houses. My head told me he had to follow his conscience that heard in one hundred days of retreat over two years that he was called to marriage. Even so, I still had to grieve with my heart each loss. For fifteen years we had traveled together to forty countries giving retreats and had written nine books on healing prayer. We knew each other so well that we could invariably guess what the other would order off a ten-page Chinese menu. I grew so depressed that I had dreams of crashing in an airplane and felt relieved that I was dead. I wanted to quit giving retreats, become a hermit and avoid everyone. Many of my compulsive patterns that I thought were healed, now returned. But the same things that helped me in Bolivia worked now too. Whenever I could face my loss and vulnerability and share it with another, I could grieve and find new life. For example, much healing occurred through healing prayer as I made an eight-day retreat in Dennis' empty room. I ate alone in his favorite Chinese restaurants and shared the pain with God and friends.

By this time 12 Step programs such as ACOA and Coda were widespread. They applied the 12 Steps to the problems I was experiencing. I went to ACOA and worked through the ways my loss of Dennis was like the loss of my brother, John, who died of bronchitis when I was seven. At Coda I discovered how I was struggling to be a separate person and needed to care for myself rather than find life only in Dennis' shadow. I also discovered I had been looking down on Dennis, assuming I was more virtuous than he because I was continuing to choose religious celibacy. Finally, I realized that Dennis had to follow his conscience and that his choice of marriage was just as virtuous as my choice of celibacy. I had thought Coda was just for dependent underachievers who felt shamefully inferior to others. I learned it is also for independent overachievers like myself who felt shamelessly superior to others. The healing of codependence happens only when I become interdependent and quit relating to others as one-up or one-down and begin to acknowledge both my own strengths and my vulnerability.[6] Between 12 Step meetings and healing prayer, I received so much new life that within three months I could give the retreats I had dreaded. I had great creative energy to write new talks and now look forward to writing this book.

Two years ago was again a year of major changes: moving to Minneapolis and leaving Omaha friends after thirteen years, a new part-time job of supervising spiritual directors (in addition to working with Dennis and Sheila), and working with people who have reached impasses with their therapists. With changes in work, community, and nearly everything else, I scored 385 on the Holmes-Rahe scale measuring stressful changes. Dr. Holmes found that those with a score of 300 or more had a major illness rate of 80% in the next two years.[7] Yet I didn't even get a cold after years of an unending series of colds. I believe my immunological response is strong simply because I have learned to deal with stress through sharing with my Thursday morning support group. I now know that 12 Step recovery is for everyone and that it empowers me to live a healthy, balanced life.

WHEN DID YOU MOST BELONG?

My hand still feels cold as I (Dennis) just came in from gathering a few stones from a babbling clear brook near our home. I knew that this brook expedition was just what I needed to get me over the "writer's block" I experienced earlier today. I knew the brook was the answer because a little over a year ago I experienced the same "writer's block." As usual Sheila and Matt were getting a million insights and turning out page after page. No matter how hard I tried to write, I didn't get much past the blank page in front of me. Feeling terrible, I began doing everything imaginable to help me write. I exercised, and when that didn't work I napped, and when that didn't work I tried something else. The results came up the same: a blank page.

Finally, I decided to quit and watch the news on TV. One news story was about a stripper from Texas. She threatened to sue her employers because, at age forty-one, they weren't going to allow her to strip anymore. During the news report she started dancing and stripping. I thought, "My God! On TV! Where is she going to stop? Do more!" Finally I thought, "You know, I'm feeling pretty strongly about this idiotical thing." So I stopped for a moment to listen to my feelings. My feelings felt like this little guy with big huge eyes popping out of even more massive eye glasses. So I did what I usually do and asked the little guy, "What is it that you really need and want?" As soon as I asked the question, I knew the answer. He wanted time to be with things just as they naturally are.

I walked down to the babbling clear brook, put my hand in it, and started to splash its cool water on my face. As the drops fell from my face, I felt as if scales were disappearing. I became present to the sounds of the water, to the position of each rock, to the feel of the bubbly stream gushing against my hand. On the way home I felt the tingling of newly enlivened body cells. Even though I was retracing my steps, this time I noticed the crocuses that I missed before. All my ideas were becoming clearer. When I sat down to write, the pages flowed.

Often since that day the brook has given me the opportunity to come home to myself, to get back a sense of belonging. I not only return to the brook on days like today when I experience "writer's block," but anytime when I need a sense of clarity. For instance, sometimes I have difficulty with decisions, such as when we are making up a schedule and have many options. The brook has planned many schedules for me.

At almost every 12 Step meeting, we hear testimonies such as mine about what helped a person recover a sense of belonging. Recovering people will repeat the same testimony again and again, meeting after meeting. Such people appreciate what Bill W. knew, that these memories need to be carried in our hearts because they hold the solution to future crises. I cannot afford to forget the brook.

As important as the memory about the brook is for me, that is probably not the story of belonging I would share first at a recovery meeting. The memory of most belonging and healing in my life occurred just before my 18th birthday in November, 1962. But to understand that moment, you would have to understand how its opposite, a sense of not belonging, filled my adolescence.

My deepest feelings of not belonging occurred around the time of my senior prom. I did not like girls. Now that's nothing against girls because I didn't like guys or myself either. The reason for all this is that early on I became addicted to self-hatred because of a very rigid, moralistic Roman Catholic background. Everything became a major sin. For instance, every summer we went on a trip for about three weeks. The first day on one of those trips, we stopped at a gas station. I walked inside and saw a calendar with a nude woman. I thought, "Oh my God. Now I have committed a mortal sin. It's going to be at least three weeks before I can go to confession. If we're in a car accident on this trip, and if I die I'm going straight to hell." It was awful. I was so scrupulous. Because of that I didn't like myself and I didn't like anybody else either.

So, when the time came for the senior prom, I had nobody to invite. But I was lucky because the girls' school had their senior prom three weeks before ours. When prom time arrived, one of the girls, Kathy, who was just as unpopular as I was, had no other choice but to invite me to her prom. I was the only guy in school who didn't have a date yet. In desperation she called me and said, "Dennis, how would you like to go to my senior prom?" Although I didn't want to go I decided, "I will go to hers and kind of practice up. Then I can invite her to mine." So, I said, "Yes." I endured her prom and gave thanks when the night finally ended.

After procrastinating for many days, I could not put off any longer inviting Kathy to my senior prom. I figured, "If I call her up, maybe she won't be there. Then I can tell everybody that I tried." I had bad luck. She answered the phone. For ten minutes nonstop, she told me how her evening with me was the best of her life, etc. . . . I honestly didn't know what Kathy was talking about.

When she finally stopped to breathe, I said, "Kathleen, how would you like to go to my senior prom?" She answered, "Dennis, I'd love to go to your senior prom. Let me check with my mother." As she put the phone down, I could hear the whole conversation. Her mother was surprised and thrilled that anybody would invite this child to the senior prom. She had good reason to be surprised, believe me. Her mother kept urging, "Go! I'll buy you anything you need." Finally, Kathleen came back to the phone and said, "I'm sorry. My mother says I have to babysit. I can't go to your senior prom."

I felt so sad. But I wasn't surprised because I didn't like myself, and I figured no one else did either. One reason I entered the Jesuits is because word was not out yet that lay people with a soul like mine could be saved. The Jesuits had the longest training and I figured I needed all the help I could get. Although I've always been grateful that I joined the Jesuits, my motives for entering weren't the best.

A few months after entering the Jesuits, my life changed radically. During a thirty-day retreat, the novice director instructed us to make a general confession of all the sins in our lives. I wrote eight pages, in the tiniest writing. I gave them to the priest and hoped he'd read them during his leisure time and come back and give me absolution. Instead, he told me to share with him everything that I was really sorry about in my life.

It took me over thirty minutes, but what I most remember is this: at the end of it, the priest stood up and gave me a hug. I was shocked. I had expected the usual sermon about how I had disappointed God and how I needed to make up my mind and try harder or I would ultimately suffer the painful consequences of hell. Holding those eight pages in my hand, I knew I had no guarantee that I would change because, as a scrupulous person, I had confessed those same things many, many times. But I had never before experienced a hug that so assured me that at least this person and even God loved me whether I ever changed or not. I went back to my room and cried and cried grateful tears. In the midst of those tears, I promised aloud to God and myself that I would go anywhere, any time to help another experience such a transformation.

That hug filled me with a sense of belonging that changed my life. From then until now, I have loved myself. I wouldn't trade myself with anybody. Since then, I also have felt an almost automatic, effortless love for others. In Lk 7:38 a woman, reported to be a prostitute, washed Jesus' feet with her tears and wiped them with her hair. Jesus said, "That woman can love me a lot because she's been forgiven a lot." Like a person forgiven a debt of five million instead of just five, in that hug I received what even today I consider the core of my identity: a person who can love a lot because he has been forgiven a lot. That hug and deep sense of belonging changed the addicted part of me that I hated the most and used to call "Terrible Me" into the gifted part of me that I now treasure the most and call "Loves A Lot." In Chapter Four we will focus on how a sense of belonging can change an addiction into a gift.

The Twelve Steps in My Life

When I was trying to discern whether to marry Sheila, my spiritual director asked me to write down daily the moments in my Jesuit life when I most belonged. I also began going to 12 Step meetings as I wanted in this decision making process to deal honestly with the addictions in my life. When I first went to a meeting, I had never previously worked the 12 Steps. What surprised me most was that the moments in my Jesuit life of deepest belonging which I had just written down seemed to correspond to the 12 Steps. For instance, the general confession that I just described is much like Step 5. Perhaps the moment each day when I most had the sense of belonging, our evening review of the day that I did with Sheila and Matt, was like Step 10. The correlation between my moments of belonging and the 12 Steps was evident all the way through Step 12 that talked about carrying this message to others. I had gone to some 40 countries mainly to help others experience those moments which the 12 Steps describe so well. Thus when I returned home from my first 12 Step meeting, I wrote in my journal:

> I joined 12 Step recovery back in 1962 when I thought I was joining the Jesuits. At that time I admitted that because of my addiction to self-hatred and to what I perceived as a sexual addiction, my life had become unmanageable. Only a higher power could save me. Especially through the general confession, I turned my life over to that higher power and asked that all my defects be removed. During my twenty-seven years as a Jesuit, I have made a daily inventory of my life and improved my conscious contact with God through prayer and meditation. I have tried to carry this spiritual awakening to others in 40 countries.

In that paragraph, I tried to express an appreciation for the genius of Bill W., whose 12 Steps contain what had helped me most in the previous twenty-seven years of my life. Although most of the turning points in my life came from having experienced one of the 12 Steps, I had a few other breakthroughs that, at first, didn't seem so explicit in the Steps. But later, after reading the Steps and Bill W.'s other writings more closely, I found that his writings touched on even these turning points. Perhaps Bill W. only needed more time to express the breadth of his vision. We became excited about writing this book to show first, the genius of the original 12 Steps, and secondly, some ways to experience each Step in an even more healing way.

Before starting the Steps, we want to allow you to recall your moments of belonging as we have. Healing happens at recovery meetings whenever we do this.

HEALING PROCESS

1. Take a few deep breaths as if breathing from the bottom of your toes up through your legs, your abdominal muscles, and your chest.

2. Place your hand on your heart and ask God as you understand God to bring to your heart a moment in your life when you felt that you really belonged. Perhaps it was the moment you fell in love, got married or held your first child, or a moment of forgiveness like my general confession, or a moment with nature such as mine at the brook. Let your whole self bask in that moment and breathe in again the sense of belonging.

3. If you wish, ask God as you understand God to bring to your heart the moment today when you felt like you most belonged. Maybe it was the way someone greeted you, or a letter you received, or finishing a project into which you put all that you had to give. Share with God in a sentence or two what was special about that mo-

ment. Breathe in from the bottom of your toes and allow the sense of belonging that you experienced then to fill you once more.[a]

---

a) If you had any difficulty with this process, see pages 33–35.

Are You Getting Stuck?

In the prayer process at the end of the preceding section, we invited you to recall your experience of belonging. Each chapter that follows will suggest a different process to help you get in touch with your own experience. We began with a positive memory of belonging, because it is the strength that comes from recalling how we have been loved that empowers us to eventually face hurts and move through them in a healing way.

For some, the processes we use are welcome opportunities to go within, and even occasions for transforming moments of healing. For others, however, such inner work may be frightening. Our friend Diana, a gifted therapist who treats many abuse victims, told us,

> When people come to your retreats, you create a non-shaming atmosphere in which they feel safe. They know it's ok if there's a prayer process they can't do, or if they don't experience any dramatic healing. In a book, you need to write something that will help people feel as safe as they do in your presence.

Our purpose here is to take Diana's advice and communicate to you that whatever you experience is ok. Each of us is in a different place in our process of growth, depending upon how wounded we have been, how much inner work we have done, and how much support we have in our current life. Some people, like Dennis and Matt, come from a basically affirming home and have always experienced a basic sense of self, despite hurts and traumas. Others, like Sheila, were profoundly unaffirmed in childhood and have had to recover a basic sense of self. As Sheila will share in Chapter Four, it is difficult to be lovingly present to oneself in personal prayer processes until that basic sense of self has been restored.

Sometimes a prayer process suggests imagining ourselves in a particular scene. When we have done this at retreats, a few people have always responded, "But I never see anything!" For those who have difficulty visualizing, it may be helpful to know that imagination can use all of the senses. For some it is more helpful to imagine sounds or to get the felt sense of something than it is to imagine through visualization.

Some of the prayer processes here invite you to get in touch with early childhood memories. For those of us who have difficulty recalling our childhood, we can ask ourselves, "How do I long to be loved and nurtured?" Our longings will tell us what we needed and did not receive. We can also ask ourselves, "How do I treat others in my life today, e.g., my own children?" This will reveal to us how we were treated, since we tend to treat others as we have been treated or in exactly the opposite way out of fear. Healing brings a balanced freedom to treat others in an appropriate and caring way.

Some of the stories that follow involve sudden breakthroughs in healing, and it may sound as if we *should* be able to grow rapidly. In fact, however, growth is a process and the "sudden breakthrough" sometimes follows many times of feeling stuck. If you have difficulty or feel stuck at any point in this book, we hope you will trust that your inner self knows when you are ready for the next step in growth. Meanwhile, we encourage you not to run from the stuckness but instead allow yourself to be loved in it. Maybe you can best love those stuck places by sharing them with a friend. Perhaps you will want to go for a walk, take a hot bath, work in the garden or go to a 12 Step meeting. Do whatever helps you to feel loved just as you are, without trying to fix or change yourself.

There is no right or wrong way to do the prayer processes in this book. What heals is not doing the Steps or processes "right," but rather allowing yourself to be loved regardless of what happens. As Bill W. said, "Only love can heal."[1]

CHAPTER THREE

How Do Addictions Begin?

NAMING OUR ADDICTIONS

When we (Dennis and Matt) first heard about addictions, we thought we didn't have any because, after all, we come from a relatively healthy family. We don't know any other parents who love and enjoy their children more than ours do. We like watching our eighty-year-old parents take their grandchild, David, fishing or read him a bedtime story. That's because they enjoy it just as much as they enjoyed doing it with us almost half a century ago. The joyful sense of connectedness and belonging we feel at these times forms the deepest core of every human being. Yet, recently we have discovered how our addictions disconnect us from that core. In recognizing our addictions, we see that, like ourselves, probably every human being and every family has addictions. Eating with five-year-old David helped us both to discover this and to begin naming our addictions.

One day we took David's family to a buffet that had an entire table of desserts. We helped ourselves to the salad bar and sat down to eat. But David wanted to explore the whole buffet, so his parents turned him loose. We knew that if either of us were a five-year-old turned loose at this buffet, we would head straight for the dessert table and pile our tray high.

When David returned, he had piled his tray high as we expected. But what surprised us was that he had only one dessert. He had piled his tray high with healthy things, like broccoli. So we asked our sister, Mary, how she had raised such a healthy child. Mary said, "For years I tried to lose weight without success. Finally, I began asking myself two questions: 'Am I really hungry?', and if so, 'What would I enjoy eating?' " She realized that often she ate even though she wasn't hungry. She ate too much because she wasn't enjoying each food. She shared with us the foods that she didn't really enjoy, such as watermelon. We couldn't understand how anyone could not enjoy watermelon. Nevertheless, when she began to ask herself those two questions and to eat only when she was hungry and only what she would most enjoy, she lost all her extra weight.

When David came along, Mary taught him to ask himself the same two questions. She told us, "David discovered that he doesn't particularly like sweets and many times he skips desserts. Although he doesn't like everything, he always eats plenty of healthy foods."

What Mary told us about David is what child specialists from the traditional Dr. Benjamin Spock to current day psychotherapist Jane Hirchmann are also saying. Children have an "inborn mechanism that lets them know how much food and which types of food they need for normal growth and development."[1] Clinical experience shows that when parents trust their child's inborn mechanism and legalize all foods, the child may turn to "junk foods" at first, but in a relatively short time, will lose interest. Children like David, who are trusted to choose their own foods and to eat only when they are hungry, "eat healthfully." They "live comfortably with their bodies and grow up free of obsessions about food and weight."[a]

---

a) Evidence from the study of addictions suggests that this inborn mechanism can be thrown off through addiction to a harmful substance (e.g., sugar, alcohol, tobacco) and the body may need a period of withdrawal and recovery before its natural sense of what it needs can function again.

A few days later we were sitting at our parents' picnic table with David. With great care, our dad had picked his home grown beets and prepared them with his favorite German recipe. David had tried Dad's beets many times before. Dad was about to serve David beets when David said, "I don't want any. I hate beets." But Dad continued serving them anyway, while telling David, "You don't hate beets. You don't hate anything. Beets build strong muscles. Mature boys eat their beets." Even though David probably had no idea what "mature" meant, he bent over and shoveled the beets into his mouth.

In choosing not to confront Dad but rather to eat his beets and thereby swallow his pain, David opened himself to the same eating addiction Mary had. In saying this, we are not blaming Dad or David. Dad was doing what he thought best. He was probably treating David as he had been treated. Dad was raised in a strict German culture where often a crying child was left to cry so it would "learn self-discipline." In that culture it was assumed that generally children could not be trusted to know what they needed. As for David, eating those beets was probably the best way he knew at the time to belong to his grandfather. If such behavior continued, David could easily develop an eating addiction, since addictions originate in our best attempts to belong.[2]

Despite our best intentions, addictions can develop whenever we, like David, choose a way to belong that separates us from our own reality. By asking his body those two questions before eating, David had learned that his body will never lie. But Dad told David to eat beets and distrust his own body. "You don't hate beets," told David not only to distrust his body but also to deny his feelings and thoughts about beets. To the extent David did that, he separated himself from his own reality. He became split inside and no longer belonged to his true self. That split can deepen whenever he is again told, "Don't trust, don't feel, don't think," which are the messages at the core of every addiction.[b] As the split deepens inside, David may well look outside himself for an escape from the pain of losing his real self. Perhaps, like Mary, David will learn to eat (even foods he doesn't enjoy) as a way of swallowing painful feelings. An addiction is any substance or process that we consistently use to escape from our own reality, especially painful feelings. Bill W. described this in alcoholics, who he said were like a "man who, having a headache, beats himself on the head with a hammer so that he cannot feel the ache."[3]

When David bent over to eat his beets, I (Dennis) recalled my earliest childhood memory, of playing airplane with Dad. Airplane also had to do with beets. Like David I hated them. The airplane was a forkful of beets which Dad whizzed and circled through the air with the "rrrr rrrr" sound of its sputtering motor until it miraculously landed safely in the landing strip of my mouth. Airplane meant that the first, third and last forkfuls of beets landed in Dad's mouth, and only the second and fourth forkfuls in mine. Thus, rather than denying my reality by bending over and eating my beets as David did, I denied my reality by playing airplane with Dad. To me "airplane" meant "people pleasing," and the addiction I still deal with most is what I call "Peace at Any Price." Peace at Any Price, who proudly holds up his clean plate after playing airplane with Dad, reveals himself in many addictive symptoms in my life. I find in myself, for example, what psychiatrist Dr. Gerald May calls "attraction addictions" (e.g., seeking approval and being nice), and "aversion addictions" (e.g., avoiding conflict and anger). (See page 45.)

That day at the picnic table with David, I acted out of my

---

b) Like all children, David needs guidance in situations where his sense of his own and other people's limits is undeveloped or where he has insufficient information about life. But in the case of food, David's own body gives him the healthy answers he needs.

Peace at Any Price addiction. Even though I had lost my appetite during the exchange between David and Dad, I kept eating my beets. I felt sad, angry, and hurt, yet I said nothing, hoping that the storm would blow over. The way out of my addiction would have been to face the conflict and say something like, "Dad, when you insist that David eat beets, I feel sad, angry and hurt. I need you to stop insisting or I need to take David inside to eat." Maybe that would have freed my dad to respond with something like, "David, I got angry and carried away. I'm sorry. I didn't realize how important it was to me that you try my beets. But even more important to me is that you know I trust you to know what you want. If you don't like those beets, you don't have to eat them." If we had done that we would have both trusted what we were feeling and thinking and allowed David to do the same. We would have helped David discover with us how to create a less addictive environment where everyone can think, feel, and trust.

The beet story happens many times a day in most of our lives. Before entering recovery, I frequently told Sheila, "You shouldn't feel that way." I still often tell Matt exactly what he should think about my latest golden insight. One of the most common messages we hear, whether over TV or from another, is, "Don't trust, don't think, and don't feel," Perhaps that is why Gerald May says,

> Addiction is any compulsive, habitual behavior that limits the freedom of human desire . . . all people are addicts . . . addictions to alcohol and other drugs are simply more obvious and tragic addictions than others have. To be alive is to be addicted, and to be alive and addicted is to stand in need of grace.[4]

As Bill W. said, "The whole world is on a terrific dry bender!"[5] Whether the symptom be overeating or Peace at Any Price, we all have addictive ways of escaping the painful parts of our reality and thus ways we are in need of grace. To receive that grace, it helps to name the addictive places within us where we most hunger for it.

Opposite is Gerald May's list of common addictions.[6] There are probably many more, since there are as many different addictions as there are ways to escape from a painful reality of our life. Thus, you may wish to begin by remembering your "beet story," what you did as a child or perhaps even do compulsively now in order to escape painful feelings. You may be surprised to find a few addictions that even Gerald May has yet to discover.

THE 12 STEP REVOLUTION:
FOCUSING ON EMOTIONAL ISSUES

Gerald May's chart includes two types of addictions: process addictions and substance addictions. We have struggled with process (non-substance) addictions, such as Matt's angry perfectionism, Sheila's compulsive fear, or Dennis' addiction to seeking approval and avoiding conflict. But we haven't struggled with ingestive, substance addictions that need specific treatment for the physiological factors involved (abstinence from drugs, medical care during withdrawal, correcting biochemical imbalances, etc.).[7] Therefore we will stay with our experience and in this book focus on the emotional component that is involved in any addiction. In the story of David, we described how this emotional component develops. Under "emotional component" we include social and cultural factors related to our sense of belonging, such as, in the case of an alcoholic, whether his or her friends are found only in bars and whether that person's ethnic group has a history of alcoholism.

Because we are focusing on the emotional component, we will deal primarily with what is sometimes called "Stage II Recovery," in contrast to "Stage I Recovery."[8] Stage I Recovery involves

ATTRACTION ADDICTIONS

Anger	Drinking	Intimacy	Relationships
Approval	Drugs	Jealousy	Responsibility
Art	Eating	Knowledge	Revenge
Attractiveness	Envy	Lying	Scab picking
Being good	Exercise	Marriage	Seductiveness
Being helpful	Fame	Meeting	Self-image
Being loved	Family	expectations	Self-improve-
Being nice	Fantasies	Memories	ment
Being right	Finger	Messiness	Sex
Being taken	drumming	Money	Shoplifting
care of	Fishing	Movies	Sleeping
Calendars	Food	Music	Soft drinks
Candy	Friends	Nail biting	Sports
Cars	Furniture	Neatness	Status
Causes	Gambling	Parents	Stock market
Chewing gum	Gardening	Performance	Stress
Children	Golf	Pets	Sunbathing
Chocolate	Gossiping	Pimple squeezing	Suspiciousness
Cleanliness	Groups	Pistachio nuts	Talking
Coffee	Guilt	Pizza	Television
Comparisons	Hair twisting	Politics	Time
Competence	Happiness	Popcorn	Tobacco
Competition	Hobbies	Popularity	Weight
Computers	Housekeeping	Potato chips	Winning
Contests	Humor	Power	Work
Death	Hunting	Psychotherapy	Worthiness
Depression	Ice cream	Punctuality	
Dreams	Images of God	Reading	

AVERSION ADDICTIONS

Airplanes	Commitment	Mice	Public speaking
Anchovies	Conflict	Needles	Rats
Anger	Crowds	Open spaces	Rejection
Animals	Darkness	Pain	Responsibility
Being:	Death	People of	Sex
Abnormal	Dentists	different:	Sharp instruments
Alone	Dependence	Beliefs	Slimy creatures
Discounted	Dirt	Class	Snakes
Fat	Disapproval	Culture	Spiders
Judged	Doctors	Politics	Storms
Over-	Embarrassment	Race	Strangers
whelmed	Evil spirits	Religion	Success
Thin	Failure	Sex	Tests
Tricked	Fire	People who are:	Traffic
Birds	Germs	Addicted	Tunnels
Blood	Guilt	Competent	Vulnerability
Boredom	High places	Fat/Thin	Water
Bridges	Illness	Ignorant	Writing
Bugs	Independence	Neat/Messy	
Cats	Intimacy	Rich/Poor	
Closed-in			
spaces			

abstinence from the addiction, e.g., from alcohol, drugs, etc. Important as this is, it does not mean the underlying emotional patterns have been healed.[c] People who are stuck in this stage are sometimes spoken of as "thinking alcoholically" and "on a dry drunk." They commonly substitute addictions, e.g., smoking or overeating for alcohol. Stage II Recovery, what Bill W. called "true sobriety" or "serenity," involves embracing a new way of life that is emotionally and spiritually healthy.[9]

Bill W. recognized the emotional component in addiction when he linked his first drink with his desire to belong. The most obvious evidence that Bill W. saw addiction as first an emotional/ spiritual problem is his solution: the 12 Steps that deal entirely with emotional and spiritual issues. It is surprising that there is no step such as, "I will get rid of all my alcohol," or "I will stay away from those who are drinking." Such steps would focus on the physical avoidance of alcohol. Instead the whole purpose of the 12 Steps is a spiritual awakening. Bill knew that when this occurs, sobriety will happen automatically.[10]

Looking at the emotional roots has created a revolution in understanding addiction. For example, 61% of those in Overeaters Anonymous (OA) come from dysfunctional, alcoholic families.[11] An OA therapist told us the key to her recovery was realizing why she often awoke at 4 A.M. with hunger that led to refrigerator raids. As she listened to her hunger she heard her inner child who felt fear because her abusive, alcoholic father would often return at 4 A.M. She also felt shame because, like virtually all children, she blamed herself for the abuse. As she dealt with her fear and shame, she was able to stop overeating.

---

c) A.A. has an acronym, "HALT" (Hungry, Angry, Lonely, Tired) for recognizing the vulnerable states that trigger relapse. While in these states we are more easily overwhelmed by underlying emotional issues and more likely to escape unresolved pain through addictive behaviors. While hunger and tiredness may be physiological triggers, anger and loneliness are more obviously emotional factors that relate to our sense of belonging.

Similar emotional hurts underlie other addictions. For example, 83% of sex addicts were sexually abused in childhood, 73% physically abused, and 97% emotionally abused. [12]

Dr. Phillip Mac is Co-Director of the Chemical Dependency Institute (CDI) that treats those in chronic pain who have become addicted to their pain medication. He stresses treatment for the root of the pain: the emotional traumas of childhood. All CDI's clients in the chronic pain program's first year of operation were adult children of dysfunctional families. Ninety percent of them were survivors of emotional, physical or sexual abuse.

> Children from dysfunctional families have so much psychic pain that often it becomes much easier for them to deal with it on a physical plane. And so their emotional problems shift into physical problems. . . . Once you get the people off the drugs, the emotional trauma recurs . . . a lot of people are afraid of that. They can't handle it. . . . Before you can move on, a lot of those past experiences need to be healed. [13]

What is at the core of the "psychic pain" that fuels addiction? Many believe it is the feeling of shame. Shame caused the awkward and socially inept Bill W. to take his first drink. Shame caused David, with downcast eyes, to shovel another forkful of beets into his mouth. [14] Gershen Kaufman says, "Addictions are rooted in internalized scenes of shame," [15] and John Bradshaw writes:

> I've been an active part of the recovering community for 22 years. I've counseled some 500 alcoholics and run the Palmer Drug Abuse Program in Los Angeles for four years, having been a consultant to that program for ten years prior to that. In all those years I've never seen anyone who did not have abandonment issues and internalized shame, along with their physical addiction. [16]

Pat Carnes, who has treated thousands for sexual addiction, agrees:

Shame emerges from addiction. Shame causes addiction. Whichever way the shame is flowing, whether consequence or cause, it rests on one key personal assumption: Somehow I am not measuring up. This belief starts early in life.[17]

Carnes studied the families of sex addicts and found that only 2.5% came from healthy families, compared with 47% of non-sex addicts.[18] Using a system of sixteen equally possible family types, he found that 68% of the addicts and 62.5% of the coaddicts came from only one of the sixteen types: the rigid, disengaged family. This family type had the most rigid rules (in a futile attempt to create unity) and the least sense of emotional belonging. Such families with little sense of belonging raise shame-based children, who grow up feeling overwhelming shame from never measuring up to the rigid standards of perfection that bring acceptance. Fearful of rejection, they avoid being close and feel the shame both of being inadequate and of never belonging.[19] This shame triggers the five-step addictive cycle described by Carnes that we express in belonging language.[20]

CARNES ADDICTIVE CYCLE	IN OUR WORDS
1) I am basically a bad, unworthy person (shame).	1) I don't belong (come home) to my true self so I am a bad, unworthy person (shame).
2) No one would love me as I am.	2) I don't belong to anyone else.
3) My needs are never going to be met if I have to depend on others.	3) I have *no* real way to belong and meet my needs.
4) The addictive process or substance is my most important need.	4) The addictive, false way of belonging is my most important need.

| 5) I am bad because the addiction is my most important need. | 5) I am bad because the addictive way of belonging is my most important need. |

We break out of this addictive cycle when our emotional hurts get healed by a love so deep it can penetrate and melt away the triggering shame. Love that calls us to belong to our true selves, others, God, and the universe is like sunshine that removes the shame entombing us. A wise person said: "The sun will remove the coat when the wind cannot."

PROCESS: GETTING TO KNOW OUR ADDICTIONS

The first step in recovery is getting to know our own addictions. Take some time to reflect on the following questions and share them with your higher power and/or with a friend.

1. What addictions do you recognize in yourself?
2. When are you most vulnerable to your addictions? (E.g., when you are hungry, angry, lonely, tired, frightened, overworked, etc.)
3. Can you identify feelings of shame in those times when you are most vulnerable to your addictions?
4. When are you least vulnerable to your addictions?
5. In light of all this, what do you need from your higher power or from a friend? Are you comfortable asking for what you need?

12 Steps and 12 Reflections

In this book, we have integrated the 12 Steps (originally written in 1938) with recent developments in spirituality and psychology. For example, we've expanded the Steps to include how addictive patterns are caused by childhood losses, and the need to grieve those losses and have them restored whenever possible. We have also added an emphasis on the positive, such as including gifts and strengths in the inventory.

We have taken each step and looked at it first through the eyes of Bill W. and his immediate followers. Then, we have looked at the same step through our own eyes, in light of contemporary spirituality and psychology. As we look through our own eyes, we see a different aspect of each Step that we have expressed as the Reflections below.[a] We do not mean these Reflections as substitutes for the Steps, but instead as additional ways of looking at them, somewhat like shining them through a prism and seeing new ways in which the light is refracted.

We feel some fear that our Reflections might offend those who perceive us as rewriting the Steps. Bill W. felt a similar fear:

> As to changing the steps themselves, or even the text of the A.A. book, I am assured by many that I could certainly be excommunicated if a word were touched. . . .
>
>   As time passes, our book literature has a tendency to get

---

a) Thanks to Jack McGinnis, who helped us write these Reflections.

more and more frozen—a tendency for conversion into something like dogma. This is a trait of human nature which I'm afraid we can do little about. We may as well face the fact that A.A. will always have its fundamentalists. . . .[1]

Our hope is that you will share Bill's open-hearted and courageous awareness that, "we know only a little. God will constantly disclose more to you and to us."[2] As you spend time with the Steps and our Reflections in this book, we encourage you to write your own Reflections to express the special way the light of the 12 Steps is refracted in your heart.

12 STEPS[b] & 12 REFLECTIONS

STEP 1:   We admitted we were powerless over alcohol—that our lives had become unmanageable.

STEP 2:   Came to believe that a power greater than ourselves could restore us to sanity.

---

b) The 12 Steps are reprinted and adapted with the permission of Alcoholics Anonymous World Services, Inc. Permission to reprint this material does not mean that A.A. has reviewed or approved the contents of this publication or that A.A. agrees with the views expressed herein. A.A. is a program of recovery from alcoholism. Use of the 12 Steps in connection with programs and activities which are patterned after A.A. but which address other problems does not imply otherwise.

In accordance with A.A.W.S. guidelines, the 12 Steps above are unaltered from their original form. Thus we have used the word "alcohol" in Step 1 and "alcoholics" in Step 12. In the rest of this book, the 12 Steps will be presented in such a way that any other addiction can be substituted for alcoholism. We will also avoid sexist language whenever possible, e.g., by substituting "God" for "Him" or "His" in the 12 Steps. This is consistent with a current movement within many 12 Step groups toward more inclusive language. We will not alter other direct quotes from Bill, but in our own writing we will avoid sexist language for God.

STEP 3:   Made a decision to turn our will and our lives over to the care of God *as we understood him.*

STEP 4:   Made a searching and fearless moral inventory of ourselves.

STEP 5:   Admitted to God, to ourselves, and to another human being the exact nature of our wrongs.

STEP 6:   Were entirely ready to have God remove all these defects of character.

STEP 7:   Humbly asked him to remove our shortcomings.

STEP 8:   Made a list of all persons we had harmed, and became willing to make amends to them all.

STEP 9:   Made direct amends to such people wherever possible, except when to do so would injure them or others.

STEP 10:   Continued to take personal inventory and when we were wrong promptly admitted it.

STEP 11:   Sought through prayer and meditation to improve our conscious contact with God *as we understood him,* praying only for knowledge of his will for us and the power to carry that out.

STEP 12:   Having had a spiritual awakening as the result of these steps, we tried to carry this message to alcoholics, and to practice these principles in all our affairs.

REFLECTIONS

Reflection on Steps 1, 2 and 3:   *When I embrace my powerless behavior I hear deep within myself the choked voice of a power greater than myself who invites me to restoration and a more profound sense of belonging through reconnecting with God's empowering energy as found in myself, others and the universe. I reconnect by treating everyone and everything as valued members of the same family.*

Reflection on Step 4:   *I made a searching and fearless inventory of all my connections and disconnections.*

Reflection on Step 5:   *I admitted to God, myself and another human being the exact nature of my life.*

Reflection on Step 6:   *I became willing to have restored in my life the losses that caused my defects of character. I experience this restoration as I grieve and heal the hurts behind those losses.*

Reflection on Step 7:   *I honestly embraced all that God has made available to me to have my hurts healed and my losses restored.*

Reflection on Step 8:   *In addition to a willingness to make amends to others, I made a list of all the ways my inner child has been hurt and became willing to make amends to that child.*

Reflection on Step 9:   *In addition to being willing to make amends to others, I made direct amends to that child wherever possible.*

Reflection on Step 10:   *I continued to remain faithful to a daily process of listening to the ways I am connected to and disconnected from myself, others, the universe and God, and followed my long-ing to deepen my sense of belonging to all.*

Reflection on Step 11: *Since I become like the God I adore, I sought through prayer and openness to life to heal my image of God so that I could be guided by God's unfolding love.*

Reflection on Step 12: *Having entered this process of restoration through deepening my sense of belonging to my real self, God, others and the universe as members of my family, I shared this with others.*

CHAPTER FOUR

Steps 1, 2 and 3

1. We admitted we were powerless over _____ that our lives had become unmanageable.

2. Came to believe that a power greater than ourselves could restore us to sanity.

3. Made a decision to turn our will and our lives over to the care of God *as we understood God.*

REFLECTION

When I embrace my powerless behavior I hear deep within myself the choked voice of a power greater than myself who invites me to restoration and a more profound sense of belonging, through reconnecting with God's empowering energy as found in myself, others and the universe. I reconnect by treating everyone and everything as valued members of the same family.

THE GENIUS BENEATH ADDICTIONS

Sometimes when I (Dennis) work the first three steps, I notice healing immediately. At other times nothing seems to happen for years. For example, in my general confession, I lived the first three steps. In writing the eight pages of my sins, I admitted that I was powerless and that my life had become un-manageable (Step 1). That confession came only a few weeks after joining the Jesuits. I joined the Jesuits because I had come to believe that a power greater than myself could restore my scrupu-lous self to sanity (Step 2). At the end of my confession, when I felt so loved by God and made the promise to follow God "any-time, anywhere," I was working Step 3. I was making a decision to turn my will and my life over to the care of God as I under-stood God. The two biggest addictions I confessed were a sexual addiction and a self-hatred addiction. While my sexual addiction lasted for almost ten more years, my self-hatred addiction was healed immediately and never returned. Since in the same confes-sion I had done all three steps with both my self-hatred and sexual addictions, why weren't they both healed in the same way?

I need to qualify how my sexual addiction did not change. The sexual behavior I had always hated most, that of being a compulsive Peeping Tom, changed as soon as I entered the Jesuits. For the next two years, I never acted out. But my addictive behav-ior stopped only because I was now in the Jesuit novitiate far out in the country and far away from women. Our celibate spirituality regarded women as a temptation. For instance, if I passed by a woman on an occasional trip to town, we had a rule that forbade me to talk to her. Another rule, "modesty of the eyes," meant that I could not even look up. Thus, for two years I did not act out my Peeping Tom addiction because I had no opportunity.

To not act out an addiction is crucial, but it isn't enough. Unless we heal the core issues of belonging which trigger addic-tions in the first place, we often just trade addictions. I traded my Peeping Tom addiction for an aversion addiction, fear of women.[1] Many alcoholics trade their drinking addiction for a smoking or eating addiction. Also, when we don't treat core issues the old addictions often return even more fiercely. That is what happened to me. After I left the novitiate to begin university study, my Peep-ing Tom addiction, now fueled by a fear of women, returned. I recall how often I felt empty and helpless as I once again turned the corner into the girls' dormitory parking lot and from the safety of my car wished that Peeping Tom could see something. For the next eight years, my Peeping Tom addiction made that empty, helpless feeling a regular part of my life. I tried everything I knew to change, but nothing worked.

Change finally came in an unexpected way. One day I noticed that for the past six months Peeping Tom hadn't acted out. I was surprised because during that time I hadn't tried anything new in order to change my behavior. Before it had been an everyday issue; for months now I had forgotten about it.

What helped Peeping Tom to change without me even trying? The only difference in my life was that I had joined the Charismatic Renewal. Two things happened there. First, people shared their life stories just as they do at 12 Step meetings. Coming from an environment where self-revelation was discouraged, I was grateful for the courage charismatics gave me to begin sharing my story. As I shared myself, much as I am doing now, many came to me for counseling. To my surprise, they trusted me with their intimate stories. Secondly, the charismatics I knew loved to hug. At first I was scared of so many hugs, but I soon liked them. I found that people became transparent to me just by the way they hugged. Like those in the counseling sessions, they were allowing me to know their real selves.

Why did this heal my addiction? What I discovered was that Peeping Tom's deepest longing had always been to know people just the way they were, with no phoniness. He had known no better way to do this than to see a person naked. Sharing inside stories with people, theirs and mine, answered in a healthy way Peeping Tom's need for belonging. I renamed "Peeping Tom," "Inside Story." Whether in counseling, in giving and receiving a hug, or in the writing I am doing now, I discovered that I have a genius to be with the "inside story" of myself or another. Behind every addiction is a genius.

For the last fifteen years I have been free of my Peeping Tom addiction. Perhaps that is because whenever I experience strong sexual feelings, I ask "Inside Story" what it needs in order to belong. (See Focusing Prayer Process on pages 80–81.) It will always tell me how I need to reconnect with God, myself, another, or the universe. For instance, I have shared my reaction to the forty-one-year-old stripper on TV. In that situation, "Inside Story" knew I needed to be with nature "just as it is." Often Inside Story tells me to cook a Chinese meal. When I cook Chinese food, I take time to touch and look at the ingredients as I prepare them for the wok. I know the "inside story" of each color, taste and texture so well that sometimes I think the vegetables and sauces are telling me what they want me to do next. Sometimes Inside Story sends me jogging so I can feel every bone and muscle in my body. Other times, Inside Story suggests that I have an intimate conversation with a friend.

My fullest experience of Inside Story happens in marriage. Sheila and I tease about how she has to place her hand over her face so that I won't know what she is thinking. Although anyone could tell by looking at her face, I am getting so good that I can even do it standing behind her. What I have always treasured most about Sheila is that she never learned, as I did, to hide her inside story.

At the core of my sexual addiction, Peeping Tom, I discovered a genius, Inside Story. As I do whatever my addiction most needs in order to regain a sense of belonging, the addiction reveals its genius, a unique but hidden capacity to give and receive love. It may seem like a long, tedious process to discover what each addiction most needs. But generally the needs of each of our addictions are so similar that when one addiction gets what it needs, so do the others. This became evident to me with my study addiction and my religious addiction.

My study addiction began in high school. I picture it as a

little guy carrying a stack of tottering books three times as tall as himself. He feels helpless as his oversized glasses begin slowly slipping down his nose. I called him "Mr. Know It." He always studied lofty subjects. Thus he never paid attention to the rhythm inside himself nor did he ever learn normal social skills, such as dancing. His addiction reached the critical stage as the computer age set in. No matter what book he read, before he could finish it a dozen other books had been published that made his book already obsolete. The longer he lived, the more behind he got. Finally, after Mr. Know It had kept me up all one night and I was exhausted, I asked, "What do you really want to know?" The answer was clear. "I want to know you." I discovered I had a genius for knowing myself. Now, with Sheila and Matt, I have written ten books. They mainly share how I have gotten to know myself and invite others to do the same. "Mr. Know It" I renamed, "Mr. Know Me."

Once we give an addiction what it needs, that does not mean it will never return. For instance, sometimes in the evening I will be reading. Suddenly, I realize that I couldn't tell you what I have read during the last half hour. Then I know that the compulsive Mr. Know It has returned. What I do is ask it what it needs in order to get back a sense of belonging. For the last five years Sheila, Matt and I have shared two questions at the end of each day: "For what am I most grateful today? For what am I least grateful?" We find this a wonderful way to reflect on our day and discover more about ourselves. Often Mr. Know It will remind me that we have skipped this process. If so, generally after sharing with Sheila and Matt I can return to reading without compulsiveness. I will remember what I am reading. As I pay attention to Mr. Know It and the ways he keeps inviting me to get to "know me," I am discovering more of my own rhythm and even that Mr. Know Me can dance.

Mr. Know It is much like Peeping Tom. Since they both

want me to know myself better, what helps one helps the other. As they helped me know myself better, I also began recovering from religious addiction.

In grade and high school I was addicted to religious practices. I began the morning with daily Mass. At lunch time I made a visit to the Blessed Sacrament. On my way home from school in the afternoon I said the Stations of the Cross. In the evening I prayed the rosary. In between times, as when I was grocery shopping, I repeated perhaps a hundred times a prayer that gave indulgences, e.g. "Jesus, Mary, and Joseph." (If you were going to hell anyway, indulgences didn't help you. But if you were lucky enough to only merit the punishment of purgatory, indulgences were good actions credited against the punishment your sins merited. "Jesus, Mary, and Joseph" was my favorite prayer because each time I said it, I merited seven years indulgence. No other four-word prayer gave such a high reward.) In the Jesuit novitiate my religious addiction took the form of blindly following religious authority. Regardless of the symptoms, religious addiction kept me from trusting myself, as I was compulsively looking outside of myself for an answer.

I picture my religious addiction as a little kid who can hardly walk because he keeps tripping over his rosary beads and his cassock, which is twenty sizes too big for him. I call him St. Dennis. One day in desperation I asked St. Dennis, "What do you want?"

St. Dennis: I want to find God.
Myself: That is pretty obvious. But you are driving me crazy. Where do you want to go to find God?
St. Dennis: Inside you.

At the core of St. Dennis' addiction was again a genius. I have a genius to discover God inside myself. I especially do this by listening to the choked voice of God at the bottom of every addiction. When I listen to that choked voice that always knows the way out, transformation happens. Terrible Me becomes Loves A Lot, Peeping Tom becomes Inside Story, Mr. Know It becomes Mr. Know Me. Each time I have listened to the choked voice within my addiction tell me what it most needs in order to belong, the message has so transformed me that I know I have heard God.

Because of the genius buried underneath my religious addiction for finding God within, I renamed "St. Dennis," "Dennis the Priest." Tad Guzie describes how I experience Dennis the Priest.

> God is not first to be found out there, in the temples on Twelfth Street or Pleasantview Avenue, but in the temple of our hearts. What was once outside is now within, so that finding God and worshiping him is completely tied up with finding ourselves.[2]

Dennis the Priest invites Terrible Me, Peeping Tom, Mr. Know It or whatever else I am feeling to listen to the choked voice of God "within the temple of their heart." At retreats as I invite others to do the same, people share with each other and give thanks for their newly discovered geniuses.

The image of people giving thanks for the genius they discover at the core of their addiction helps us to answer the question we asked at the beginning of the chapter. How come when I carefully work the first three steps does so much healing happen with one addiction and so little with another? For healing to happen, we find it helpful to add two dimensions to the first three steps: the need to embrace our addiction and the need to find a God within. In our reflection on how to experience the first three steps in the most healing way possible, we include these two dimensions.

When I embrace my powerless behavior I hear deep within myself the choked voice of a power greater than myself who invites me to restoration and a more profound sense of belonging, through reconnecting with God's empowering love as found in myself, others and the universe. I reconnect by treating everyone and everything as valued members of the same family.

Usually when 12 Step groups speak of the first three steps, they emphasize "getting rid of" rather than "embracing" our addictive behavior. They also speak of a "higher power" rather than the choked voice of God within. Although it is true that we must stop acting out and "get rid" of our addictive behavior, we find that easiest to do when our addictions are embraced. And though God is a higher power, we find that power more available when we listen to the choked voice of God within. Just what do "God within" and "embrace an addiction" mean, and how would Bill W. understand their importance?

To speak of an "inner voice" or "God within" may seem distant from 12 Step language which refers to God as a "higher power," as if God were way out there. However, Bill W. referred to God both ways. Biographer Robert Thomsen writes that "Bill W. had no hesitancy in referring to an inner voice, but in talking to others used the term higher power, life force, or any other word that the listener might be comfortable with."[3] Although Bill W. spoke about God in whatever way might help people feel most comfortable, God within is what most matched his own personal experience. Bill wrote, "We found that great reality deep down inside of us. In the last analysis it is only there that God may be found. It was so with us."[4]

Besides knowing God within, Bill W. probably would have understood what we mean by "embracing our addiction." We use the word "embrace" because what heals an addiction most is a sense of belonging. An image of this is my general confession and the hug I received at the end of it. That hug healed my self-hatred because I knew I was welcomed with my self-hatred behaviors, whether I ever changed or not. Somehow, I knew in that hug that the priest did not fear that part of me. Thus he could give it an unconditional welcome. (I believe my sexual addiction would have been healed at the same time if it had been given the same welcome. Probably my sexual addiction was not healed because the fear of sexuality in the entire Jesuit novitiate made it impossible for that priest or anyone else to welcome home that part of me.) As a scrupulous person, I had confessed my sins of self-hatred many times before with no change. But this was the first time I knew that I was loved unconditionally whether or not I ever changed. Only love and welcome heal permanently.[5]

"Embracing an addiction" means doing what helped me listen to the stories of Peeping Tom, St. Dennis and Mr. Know It. Addictions come from alienated parts of ourselves, places within where we are at war. So, I first have to ask the deepest part of myself if it is ready to stop fighting and to embrace the alienated part of myself. (If the answer is "No," I stop and listen to the story of that "No.") Once I feel a readiness, it means declaring a truce, a ceasing of any hostilities against my addiction, and a mutual agreement with my addiction to explore peace and new life.[a] "Embrace" means to give my addiction a sense of belonging, to stop treating it as an enemy and more as a possible friend with a message of peace.[6] The goal in embracing my addiction is to eventually welcome home Peeping Tom or any other addiction much as I would welcome home Sheila, Matt or a close friend. Only in such safety can my addiction share with me its story and

---

a) This does not mean I act out my addiction in destructive ways. But in this moment, my *focus* is not on ceasing to act out, but rather on embracing my whole addicted self exactly as it is, without "ifs" or conditions. Addictions come from shame, and shame comes from conditional love. What heals addictions is an embrace of unconditional love.

what it most needs in order to get back a sense of belonging. Once I hear its story, I discover its genius—its unique but hidden capacity to give and receive love.

Bill W. and psychiatrist Carl Jung understood how this happens with the addiction to alcohol. In a letter to Bill W., Carl Jung wrote that the more he listened to the stories of alcoholics, the more he understood that alcoholism was a longing for *spiritus* or Spirit: "Alcohol in Latin is *spiritus* and you use the same word for the highest religious experience as well as for the most depraving poison."[7] Jung concluded that a religious experience could rescue one from alcoholism, by giving an alcoholic the *spiritus* he or she most longed for and most needed in order to regain a sense of belonging. Bill W. recognized that alcoholics probably had a genius for this religious experience or what Bill W. preferred to call "enlightenment or higher consciousness." He wrote, "Was not their excessive use of alcohol, a perverted form of search for some measure of enlightenment or higher consciousness?"[8] Fifteen minutes of listening to stories at an A.A. meeting would tell you that Bill W. and Carl Jung were correct. Alcoholics have a genius for receiving enlightenment. And just as Bill and Jung predicted, when this enlightenment or higher power takes over the lives of alcoholics, their need for "spiritus" is satiated and their drinking stops.

Bill W. and Carl Jung did with alcoholism what I did with Peeping Tom, Mr. Know It, Terrible Me, and St. Dennis. They embraced or welcomed it until it felt safe enough to share its story. Such welcome is part of the genius of A.A. When I walk into a 12 Step meeting, I immediately feel welcomed just as I am. When I start to share my story and begin with, "I'm Dennis," everyone responds with the welcome, "Hi, Dennis." Perhaps the greatest challenge facing 12 Step recovery groups is to give that same welcome to every feeling and need beneath every addiction. Whether it be the messy sexual feelings behind a Peeping Tom addiction or the more acceptable feelings behind a St. Dennis religious addiction, every feeling beneath an addiction has a story to share. The challenge for 12 Step recovery is to address every feeling and every addiction in the same respectful way that Tradition Three addresses the "serious drinker":

> You are an A.A. member if you say so. You can declare yourself in; nobody can keep you out. No matter who you are, no matter how low you've gone, no matter how grave your emotional complications—even your crimes—we still can't deny you A.A. We don't want to keep you out. We aren't a bit afraid you'll harm us, never mind how twisted or violent you may be. We just want to be sure that you get the same great chance for sobriety that we've had.[9]

Many serious drinkers share their testimony of how they were healed when A.A. members, instead of trying to get rid of them, listened to their stories and welcomed them regardless of "how twisted or violent" they seemed. That same healing happens when we stop focusing on getting rid of our addictions or unpleasant feelings and instead welcome them to share their stories and thus reveal their genius. Addictions lose their power automatically as we release our genius, the purpose of our life. I will be indebted forever to my addictions Terrible Me, Mr. Know It, St. Dennis, and Peeping Tom for they have revealed to me the purpose of my life and given me the genius to Love A Lot, Know Me, and be Dennis the Priest who appreciates how the choked voice of God speaks through our Inside Story.

THE GENIUS BENEATH ANGER

I (Matt) am addicted to correcting and improving things to make a perfect world. Since nothing is perfect, I am frequently angry at all the imperfection I see around me and within me. Then I get angry with myself for being angry. My struggle with anger began early. Being short (now a towering 5'3"), I always ended up on the bottom of any fight. I feared that if I showed anger I might provoke a fight that I would surely lose. So I smiled and swallowed my anger with "sticks and stones will break my bones but words will never hurt me."

I also learned in my family to repress anger. As the oldest child, I could not pick on anyone younger (yet somehow it was ok for Dennis to pick on me). If Dennis did start a fight, adults always told me to shake hands rather than hit him back. For a long time afterwards, all handshakes seemed insincere. As often happens with the oldest child, my family raised me to be the responsible one. I emerged as a responsible perfectionist who learned to turn anger inward by trying harder and doing better. In high school I joined the debate team as a negative debater who could poke holes perfectly in any argument. I could criticize so well that I don't think I ever lost a debate. If I did, it was only because the judge was wrong.

Today I still struggle with anger and criticalness. When I reply to others, my first reaction is to say "But . . . " and then improve on what they said. I assume they know I agree with whatever I don't correct. Yet they have no way of reading my mind when I don't express any agreement. I've tried to change this pattern to "Yes . . . but. . . . " The "Yes" expressing agreement, however, is still a lot briefer than the disagreement coming with "but. . . . "

Discovering the Angry Person Within

Long ago I learned that trying to get rid of my anger only made it grow. Recently I have learned to listen to it through focusing.[b] When I focus on my anger, I feel my negative, angry,

---

judging energy in my body—especially in my furrowed brow and clenched fist. Then I see what image best fits that energy. I start with the energy and the image emerges out of that. For instance, I have an image of a judge inside me. He wears a black judge's coat, black suspenders and a belt to be extra sure that no one will ever catch him with his pants down. He looks like Winston Churchill with a big puffy face, and he smokes a cigar. He peers intensely through his glasses to judge what is right and wrong, good and bad. When he decides, he pounds with his gavel in his right hand. He gestures with his cigar butt in his left hand saying, "But . . . But. . . ." His name is Judge Jake.

Once Judge Jake appears, I can dialogue with him. First, I ask him what he wants. I feel his energy wanting to pound with his gavel and make decisions others must follow. He likes to pound his gavel on the table but he prefers to pound his gavel on heads to get the truth inside the person. This feels familiar, since I like the teacher's role of wanting to get truth into another. Then my voice becomes forceful, and I talk down to the other as if I were speaking to an ignorant child.

As I stay with this energy for correcting others, I feel a deeper urge to find not truth that criticizes but truth that brings life, justice, and healing. Judge Jake's desire to pound heads is at bottom a positive energy to pound home the truth that opens another to healing. As I feel new depths of my angry energy, I move further into the ways it flows with a current of giving and receiving love and life. I don't have to get rid of my anger but simply move more deeply into it from its surface destructive energy to its deepest life-giving energy.

Listening to My Judge

Moving into the loving side of my anger happens as I sit with my judge and accept that he belongs to me. As we have become friends, he has shared his story of how he has taken care of me. For example, he protected me by finding the danger before it overpowered me as the shortest kid in the neighborhood. He's also told me what he needs. Sometimes he tells me he needs a nap; he is much more upset at night when I get tired. Other times he wants to feel safe and spend more time with loving friends. Often he tells me that I am making him responsible for changing others when only they can help themselves. Sometimes he wants me to ask another person to paraphrase what I just said because Judge Jake easily feels ignored or misunderstood. Since Judge Jake has a genius for dealing with what is wrong, he can help me correct situations if I take time to feel what he wants.

I experienced this genius to correct situations recently when we gave a 12 Step retreat with Jack McGinnis. On the morning of the retreat we had agreed to leave at 8 A.M., in time to set up book tables before starting our talks at 9:00. Promptly at 8:00 I arrived at the hotel entrance but I couldn't find Jack anywhere. Judge Jake doesn't like to wait, especially when he needs every minute to be perfectly prepared. So I heard Judge Jake's anger, but that wasn't enough because I couldn't find Jack to correct the situation. When an emotion persists, I ask, "If I were not feeling this, what emotion would I be feeling?" The answer came as I felt fear underneath the anger. I was afraid we would arrive late and have to skip my talk or another's. What could I do about that? Search more for Jack. At 8:20 I found Jack calmly drinking coffee while having a sumptuous buffet breakfast with three stunning women. I said, "Jack, I've been waiting for you. How much longer do you need?" He asked for five more minutes. I went back to the car, thinking I had satisfied my judge's anger and fear. We could still start on time and someone could set up the book tables during the first talk.

But Judge Jake was still angrily pacing, so I asked again, "If I were not feeling anger or fear, what would I be feeling?" This time I felt belittling shame. I thought to myself, "Jack is having breakfast because you are not as attractive and scintillating as those three beautiful women. You can't compete with them." As I stayed with feeling shamefully shoved to the side lines, I felt an even deeper feeling. I felt abandonment at being left out of an interesting conversation and delicious buffet breakfast. What do I need to do? Judge Jake butted in by insisting I confront Jack. When Jack arrived, I said, "Jack, I felt abandoned. If this happens again, I would like you to find me so I can have breakfast too rather than just wait twenty-five minutes while you eat."

Jack responded, "I'm sorry. We said we would have breakfast first. The restaurant didn't open at 6:30 as I had thought, but rather at 8:00." That made my judge relax because I realized Jack did want to include me and assumed that I too had discovered that the restaurant didn't open until 8:00. If we hadn't cleared the air with my confrontation, I would have continued to feel abandonment. Under abandonment would have lurked my shame resulting in fear covered by anger. This anger would have come out directly or in passive aggressive behavior—maybe unconsciously being late for Jack the next time. If listening to my anger doesn't resolve a situation, usually it's because my judge is sitting on deeper layers of fear, shame and abandonment that need my care.

Looking back at what happened with Judge Jake, I understand how the first three steps give me a tool for listening to my higher power. First, in the parking lot when I let myself down into the layers of feelings beneath Jake's anger, I was admitting the depth to which "my life had become unmanageable" (Step 1). If I had not done this First Step, I might well have lashed out and hurt Jack with my denied anger.

Secondly, even to let myself down into the depths of my problem's unmanageability, I had to "believe that a power greater than myself could restore me to sanity" (Step 2). I also had to believe I had an inner sanity that could be restored. I trusted that at bottom my inner self and all my seemingly unmanageable emotions made sense. I was trusting in both an inner power (an immanent God) and a higher power (a transcendent God).

Finally, Step Three assures me that the higher power I turn my life over to is "caring." After talking with Judge Jake, I felt more like my higher power, more able to give and receive "care" in those areas of my life that were unmanageable. Therefore I believe that I heard at least part of what my higher power wanted to say to me. Without realizing it, I was doing the first three steps.

Reparenting Judge Jake

Sometimes what Judge Jake needs is not just my attention. He also needs to be with someone, perhaps Jesus or another, who is walking the path he needs to walk. For example, as I sat with Jake in my imagination during a recent retreat, he was telling me the same things I had heard previously. Then I invited my higher power, Jesus, to sit with us.[c] As Judge Jake was pounding away with his gavel, Jesus gave him a nail. This really pleased Judge Jake because he loves to nail things down and have them really hold together. Jesus then gave him another nail. This time I saw where Jesus was getting the nails. He was getting them from the person Judge Jake had been busy correcting. There was another whole step beyond loving myself and my judge, important as that was. Jesus was inviting me to love the person I was correcting and to see how that person had a nail, a special gift I needed. Rather than just tell another what was wrong, I could use their nail— their view, information, value, and uniqueness. I too needed whatever they had.

As I watched Jesus use another's nails, I wanted to do the

---

c) For a discussion of relating to Jesus in this way (what we would call "inner healing prayer"), see pp. 126ff.

same. So I asked him if Judge Jake and I could follow him around. I recalled Robert Bly's words, "A boy receives food as he stands in the shadow of his father."[10] I felt as if Jesus were reparenting Judge Jake and me as I walked in his shadow and absorbed his reactions. We walked over to the house of Simon the pharisee. I felt Jesus' desire to criticize Simon, who was condemning the woman weeping at Jesus' feet. But Jesus found Simon's nail and let Simon's discerning judge come up with the right answer to the story. "Who loves the most, the one forgiven five hundred or fifty?" Simon answered, "The one forgiven the most." "That's right, Simon! I knew you would get it right and understand that the same is happening here too."

Another day he showed me how to look at Zacchaeus and see not just a greedy tax collector. Jesus saw Zacchaeus as the host for his next great meal and as one who had a heart generous enough to give half to the poor. Gradually, Jesus reparented me as I stood in his shadow and absorbed how he channeled his anger. When I came back from that retreat I didn't know that I was any different. However, after the first day, Dennis asked me what happened on my retreat. I answered, "Why?" He said, "Because you are no longer just criticizing people and giving your view. You start with the good in what they say and build on it."

The gift of seeing the good and building on it comes and goes because my habit of angrily correcting everything is ingrained over a lifetime. Habits don't change by forcing myself to be different but by being with people I love who are walking in the direction I want to walk. So when I catch myself becoming critical, I know what I need and I take time for Jesus or someone else to reparent me again. This may be a person who isn't present, such as Gandhi whose non-violent reactions reparented me through the film, "Gandhi." Each time I watched the human waves of Gandhi's followers absorbing non-violently the blows at the Salt Works, I became less reactive to the anger around me. Usually I choose people who are physically present to reparent me. Jack McGinnis, who is less compulsive than me about being on time, is one of them.

I want to close with a funny story about how being reparented might even save us a jail sentence. An elderly woman was accosted by a young man in his mid-twenties.

> The man, roughly pushing her backwards, demanded her money.
>
> The woman quickly regained her balance and pulling herself squarely up to her full height of 5'2", said in a firm voice devoid of accusation, "Young man, what would your mother feel like if she knew you were doing this?"
>
> The young man was so taken aback that he just stood for a moment in silence. Then in a half-embarrassed voice he replied, "She'd be real hurt, real disappointed, ma'am."
>
> "I know you'd never want that to happen and neither would I," said the woman as she walked by the young man with a smile and a nod. [11]

THE GENIUS BENEATH FEAR

I (Sheila) am not addicted to any substances like drugs or alcohol. I have no obvious process addictions, such as sexual addiction or gambling. Dennis and Matt and I sometimes heard the dramatic testimonies of "big sinners." For example, "I was a cocaine addict for twenty years and I was dying in the gutter and then. . . ." In comparison, we felt dull. I remember the first time we gave a retreat with Jack McGinnis, who has been in recovery for twenty years. Jack began his first talk with, "I'm Jack and I'm a recovering alcoholic, a recovering sex addict, compulsive overeater, spending addict, codependent, adult child of two alcoholics and here's my teddy bear and I can't go anywhere without it." The people loved it. How, we wondered, can we ever even come close to Jack's ability to relate to people who struggle with addictions?

However, now that our understanding of addictive behavior has grown, I *can* identify with those who struggle with addictions. For me addiction has been more subtle than alcohol or gambling. What I have struggled with most in my life is fear. I have been stuck in (or addicted to) many compulsive behaviors (such as chronic busyness) to escape that fear. Early in my life, I was nearly always afraid, often to the point of terror. As I received healing for childhood hurts, my fear diminished and became restricted to only certain situations. Recently I have learned how, even in those situations, to feel fear in such a way that it no longer leads to so much compulsive behavior.

The situation in which I feel most frightened is when others speak critically or harshly to me. In the past, I tended to introject what they said, as if it were necessarily true, and begin speaking to myself even more harshly, using their words to beat on myself. Sometimes I would even begin to act like their negative view of me, although I knew it was not the way my real self would act.[d] Then, I would get angry at myself for doing this. That only left me feeling worse about myself and even more stuck. I would then find ways to escape my pain, such as keeping busy. I tried to change this pattern of behavior, but the harder I tried the more stuck I became.

---

d) This is an example of what Pia Mellody calls a damaged or absent internal boundary. I was unable to choose how much of other people's reality to allow inside myself, and therefore I was at the mercy of their feelings and opinions. Establishing healthy boundaries is essential to recovery. For information on internal (emotional, intellectual and spiritual) and external (physical and sexual) boundaries, see Mellody, et al., *Facing Codependence, op. cit.*, 11–21; Pia Mellody & Andrea Wells Miller, *Breaking Free* (San Francisco: Harper & Row, 1989), 316-352; Pia Mellody, *Permission to Be Precious* and *Boundaries* tape series, available from Mellody Enterprises, The Meadows, P.O. Box 1739, Wickenburg, AZ 85358.

What finally helped me most was to make friends with the fearful person within me. This happened during the two years when Denny and I were discerning our marriage. Much of our discernment process centered on external issues, such as the current laws of the Roman Catholic Church forbidding priests to marry. However, we were also working on a painful pattern in our own relationship.

The pattern involved my tendency to become frightened, stuck and self-abusive in response to criticism or harshness. Whenever this happened, I wanted to talk with Denny about it right away. I needed immediate support and care. Denny, on the other hand, tended to handle pain by avoiding it and thinking of a way to have fun. If I was upset, his solution was to forget it for now, go enjoy ourselves and maybe talk about it later. He felt angry with me if I wouldn't cooperate. I then felt angry with Denny for his seemingly uncaring response. Also, besides still being upset about whatever had originally happened, I felt even worse about myself for being so upset. Why was I so sensitive? Why couldn't I just let things go, as Denny could? At this point Denny was even more reluctant to talk, because by now I was so upset that he figured working it out would take forever. By then neither of us knew how to communicate with the other.

Denny had an image for these times. They reminded him of being in a fire station, with me pulling on his arm, as if clanging the fire station bell. I felt I had no choice but to clang the bell louder and louder, because he wasn't listening to me. So, this was the one area of our relationship where it was hard for us to understand and care for each other. I tried to change myself, but without success. What finally helped were two experiences of learning to love myself as I was. Then I changed.

Healing Fear

The first experience occurred when I again felt frightened by criticism and wanted Denny to listen to me. Denny, on the other hand, wanted to talk later. Finally, I began listening to myself. As I became present to what was going on within me, I saw an image of a little girl sitting in the dirt. She looked emaciated, and wore only a shred of a ragged shirt. I knew that she was myself. She held a stick in her hand. A large shadowy figure stood in front of her. As that person moved toward her, the child began hitting herself on the head with the stick. The closer that big person came, the harder the child hit herself.

I asked her name. She told me it was "Battered Annie." She explained to me that she was hitting herself because someone much bigger was coming toward her. If that person reached her they might hit her even harder. It was as if Battered Annie were saying to that big, shadowy figure, "If I hurt myself, then it will be done already. Maybe that will keep you from hurting me even worse."[12]

Battered Annie, using the logic of an abused child, thought that self-abuse would somehow protect her from even worse abuse from another who was bigger and stronger. I realized that she was my way of coping with the extreme verbal abuse I experienced in childhood. My mother screamed harsh words at me most of the time. I learned to scream at myself even louder in hopes that this would protect me from her. This part of myself that I had so hated—the tendency to beat on myself with harsh words whenever anyone else criticized or spoke harshly to me—was the only way I knew as a child to survive. Battered Annie was my friend. She had been trying to save my life. Although not yet free of the fearful pattern I have described, I now knew I had developed that pattern for good reasons. I no longer hated myself for it quite so much.

A short time later, again I was upset about something and I

wanted to talk about it right away. Denny wanted to go swimming. In my head, at least, I thought Denny was right. We were in Yosemite Park for only one day, with a beautiful lake in front of us. Why couldn't I just let go of what was bothering me and enjoy the day with him? Instead, we both were feeling like the fire station scene with me pulling on Denny's arm. I saw myself as being too much trouble.

I went off to be quiet and listen to myself. As I did, I felt as if someone were pulling on *my* arm. Then, in my imagination, I saw a little girl who appeared very frightened and guilty. She said her name was "Too Much Trouble" and that she was having a terrible time getting me to listen to her. She told me that whenever she needed my attention, I just got angry with her for bothering me and pushed her away. I realized I had been treating my inner self as I sometimes thought Denny treated me. I pushed myself away when I felt hurt or frightened and did not listen to myself. I saw that Too Much Trouble was doing the best she could. She could not act any differently until I loved her as she was and gave her what she needed. I felt very sorry about how I had treated this part of myself. I told Too Much Trouble that she could pull on *my* arm any time she wanted and I would not push her away anymore. I promised that I would listen to her and take care of her.

Now, when I feel hurt or frightened, I try to care for my inner self exactly as I am, without demanding that I be less sensitive. I could not do this earlier in my life; I could not parent myself because I had not yet been adequately parented. By this time, however, I had received enough care from healthy people (enough reparenting) that I could care for myself.[e] Pushing myself away was a habit I had learned as a child in a home with parents who did not know how to listen to me. It was a habit I could now give up.

---

e) See pages 89–97.

Too Much Trouble taught me that what I had thought was an outer problem between Denny and myself was really an inner problem between me and myself. From then on, that whole area of Denny's and my relationship began to change. Because I was taking care of myself on the inside, I no longer had such an urgent need to talk things out with him on the outside. When I communicated less urgency to Denny, he no longer feared that whatever had happened would take hours to work out. He, meanwhile, was working with the hurts in his life that caused him to develop a pattern of escaping painful feelings by having fun. Thus it became easy for us to negotiate whether we would talk about a problem right away or set it aside until later. As I got to know both Battered Annie and Too Much Trouble, I shared those parts of myself with Denny and he learned to help me care for them.

A friend who helped us with our discernment process told us that a healthy marriage does not require two perfectly healed people. Rather, a healthy marriage requires two people who have learned to care for their own wounded parts and for the wounded parts of each other. Thus, instead of destroying a relationship, those wounded parts become the very places where a husband and wife are vulnerable to each other and learn to cherish each other most. That is what happened for Denny and me.

Welcoming Ourselves Home

In this chapter, each of us has shared how we have welcomed home wounded and alienated parts of ourselves, listened to their story, and discovered their underlying giftedness. In the prayer that follows, we want to share with you the process we use to do this. This process is an adaptation of focusing.[13] Focusing assumes that nothing within us changes until we love it exactly as it is, without trying to fix it or change it. Hurts themselves do not cripple us. What cripples us is the way we've turned on ourselves and disowned how we feel about what happened to us.[14] Then we no longer belong to our true selves. We use addictions to fill the void where our real self should be. Healing comes when we can love and care for our disowned feelings. These feelings are stored in our bodies, and thus focusing is a way of letting the body speak to us about our true self.

The first step in this process is to get in touch with a part of yourself that needs to be listened to and cared for, as I did with my sense of being too much trouble.

Then, ask yourself if you *want* to care for that part of yourself right now. Several years ago, I would not have wanted to care for the part of myself that seemed too much trouble. In that case, perhaps I could at least have cared for *not wanting* to care for myself. The point is never to force yourself to do anything, but instead to care for yourself exactly as you are.

The next step is to create a loving atmosphere where this part of you will feel safe to speak, just as you would prepare your home for a beloved friend or open your arms to a hurting child. Ed McMahon gives an example of how creative this can be. He was working with a woman who did not want to listen to her inner reality because she so hated herself. She worked in the justice system and she believed everyone has a right to a fair hearing. Ed asked this woman if she could imagine herself in a courtroom, and if she could invite her inner self to testify. She was willing to do this, since she could not deny even her hated inner self the right to a fair hearing. As she heard her own inner story, the woman realized how unfairly she had been treating herself and felt deeply reconciled within.[15]

Once you have created a safe inner atmosphere, then become aware of how you are carrying this whole issue in your body. As I do this, the issue begins to speak to me through a word, an image, a memory or another bodily feeling. I did this with my feeling of self-hatred for being too much trouble by becoming aware that I felt as if someone were pulling on my arm. Then I let myself down into the feeling in my arm, and it spoke to me through the image of the child Too Much Trouble. As I cared for her, I felt her fear and loneliness as an ache in my chest. As I cared for that ache, it shifted and became a desire to let Too Much Trouble pull on my arm whenever she wished.

I cared for Too Much Trouble myself. I felt no need to ask for help. At other times I have invited my beloved deceased grandmother into a focusing prayer, or a friend, or Denny as I carry him in my heart. Often I want to ask Jesus to come and help me. I find Jesus' presence is healing when the desire to invite him comes from within, rather than because I think I *should*. I experience Jesus' presence whenever I am genuinely loving myself or another, whether I consciously think of Jesus or not.

After this prayer I still feared criticism and harshness. The issue had not changed. What changed was how I carried it. I no longer hated myself for my fear or tried so hard to control it. In the language of the First Step, I admitted that I was powerless[f] over fear. I have a self that is sometimes fearful and overly sensitive . . . but it's *my* self. As I love myself with my fear, I discover the genius beneath it. I have a genius for cherishing the vulnerable and fragile parts of myself and others. Because I know fear so well, I usually understand how to help a fearful person feel safe. Every issue and problem in our lives has a hidden gift or genius, discovered when we surrender to the wisdom of an inner power that is also a higher power.

---

f) I use the word "powerless" with some hesitation, because as a woman I have been taught by my culture to see myself as powerless. Like many women who share my hesitation, I find it helpful to distinguish between admitting powerlessness in general (which is *not* what Step 1 means) and admitting powerlessness over a specific addiction (which *is* what Step 1 means). Also, I appreciate Charlotte Kasl's suggestion that for women who are feeling overwhelmed by their experience of victimization, it may not be helpful to use the word "powerless" at all.[16]

FOCUSING PRAYER PROCESS[g]

1. Sit comfortably with your eyes closed. Let your awareness move down into the center of your body and notice what you feel there.
2. Get in touch with some area of your life where you feel out of control, powerless. Maybe it's an obvious addiction that seriously affects your life. Maybe it's something small but it really bothers you . . . a behavior that is hard for you to control . . . an area where you feel bad about yourself and wish you could be different.
3. Ask yourself if you *want* to listen to this part of yourself right now. Is it ok to spend some time with it? If not, care for the feeling of not wanting to spend time with this right now.
4. If it is ok to spend some time with this area of your life, take a few moments to create a loving atmosphere where it will feel safe to speak to you. For example, how would you prepare your home if your best friend were coming to visit? How would you reach out to a wounded child?
5. Now let yourself down into how this whole thing feels inside of you. Where in your body do you especially experience it? Perhaps you feel as if someone were hitting you on the head or pulling on your arm. Perhaps you feel a knot in your stomach, a lump in your throat, shaking in your legs, etc.
6. Care for this feeling and see if it wants to tell you about itself, perhaps through a word, an image or a symbol.

---

g) It may be helpful to ask another person to lead you through the steps of the focusing process. For guidance in leading another, see Edwin McMahon & Peter Campbell, *The Focusing Steps* (Kansas City: Sheed & Ward), 1991.

Perhaps it wants to come to you as a little child. Perhaps it wants to tell you its name, its history (when and how it developed) and what it needs.

7. Whatever comes, reach out to care for it without trying to change it or fix it. Or, maybe just put your hand on that part of your body in a caring way.

8. Tell this part of you that you will come back at another time and listen to it some more.

9. Before concluding, notice how your body feels compared to when you began. Are you now carrying this issue differently in your body?

Introduction to
Steps 4, 5, 6 and 7

We have often heard A.A. veterans say, "We are as sick as our secrets. To the degree we do the Fifth Step, we make the program." The Fifth Step is the heart of four steps involved in correcting wrongs: Step 4 finds the wrongs, Step 5 admits them, Step 6 becomes willing to allow God to remove them, and Step 7 asks God to remove them. Following are the original steps and our reflections on them.

4. Made a searching and fearless moral inventory of ourselves.
   I made a searching and fearless inventory of all my connections and disconnections.

5. Admitted to God, to ourselves, and to another human being the exact nature of our wrongs.
   I admitted to God, myself and another human being the exact nature of my life.

6. Were entirely ready to have God remove all these defects of character.
   I became willing to have restored in my life the losses that caused my defects of character. I experience this restoration as I grieve and heal the hurts behind those losses.

7. Humbly asked God to remove our shortcomings.
   I honestly embraced all that God has made available to me to
   have my hurts healed and my losses restored.

In our reflections we expand these steps to look not only at
wrongs but at all of life with its positive dimensions as well.
Chapter Five speaks of how a positive atmosphere of affirmation
can restore our losses and heal our disconnections. Our reflections also emphasize how healing the hurts in our lives removes
wrongdoing and character defects. Twelve Step groups such as
ACOA, Coda, Alanon, Incest Survivors Anonymous and many
others focus on healing the hurts that cripple us. Bill W. understood that recognizing our hurts as we do the inventory ". . . has
the effect of taking the ground glass out of us, the emotional
substance that still cuts and inhibits."[1] Chapter Six focuses on
how these emotional hurts are healed as we relive memories to
forgive, grieve, and restore what was lost.

CHAPTER FIVE

Steps 4, 5, 6 and 7

RESTORING OUR LOSSES THROUGH AFFIRMATION AND BELONGING

In Chapter Four, I (Sheila) mentioned the constant fear with which I lived for many years. During those years I also felt lonely, insecure, inferior, and depressed. I felt that I did not belong. My behavior included much of what Steps 5, 6 and 7 call "wrongs," "defects of character," and "shortcomings."[a] For example, as a student I often arrived late for class, after the teacher had begun speaking. I did this because my social awkwardness was so great that I felt terrified of the casual socializing that took place before class began. Also, if the teacher was a loving person, I often stayed after class and invented a question I could ask the teacher. I did this in order to get extra attention from a loving adult, and because the only time I felt confident with others was during intellectual discussions. Because of these and other behaviors, I judged myself as being immature and dependent.

Like myself, alcoholics commonly feel fearful, lonely, insecure, inferior, depressed and as though they do not belong. Bill

---

a) Bill W. used the terms "wrongs," "defects of character" and "shortcomings" interchangeably to mean the same thing. When asked why he did this, he said it was because he learned in school that a good writer did not keep repeating the same word.[1]

W. described alcoholics as fundamentally lonely people. Even before alcoholism provoked rejection from others, Bill and other alcoholics

> . . . suffered the feeling that we didn't quite belong. Either we were shy and dared not draw near others, or we were noisy good fellows constantly craving attention and companionship, but rarely getting it.[2]

When Bill summed up the character defects of the drinking alcoholic, he too used the words "immature" and "dependent." He saw these fundamental character defects as the source of the alcoholic's difficulties in life. The remedy was for the alcoholic to grow up emotionally. Bill implied that the alcoholic should root out immaturity and dependency, in the same sense that some would speak of "rooting out sin." In fact, Bill suggested that Step 4's inventory, where these defects were to be faced, be conducted according to a list of the traditional Seven Deadly Sins.[3]

While Bill understood the pain of alcoholics, it seems to us that his remedy misses something. Bill misses the fact that growing up emotionally and healing of character defects are not first of all about rooting out, but rather about building up. Although rooting out or changing destructive behavior is important, this will happen automatically as we build up a firm core sense of belonging to our true selves. Character defects or wrongs, such as my tardiness, social withdrawal and lack of honesty in asking for attention, are our best attempts to deal with the overwhelming pain of not belonging. What I or an alcoholic most needs is to build up a core sense of belonging so that such pain no longer overwhelms us. As I did this, I no longer felt compelled to arrive late for class and I began to ask straightforwardly for the attention that I needed. Bill W. no longer felt compelled to drink after he recovered a core sense of belonging in his conversion experience.

Our sense of belonging comes from what psychiatrist Dr.

Conrad Baars calls "affirmation." According to Dr. Baars, the symptoms I have described in myself and that Bill W. saw in alcoholics are the symptoms of an unaffirmed person.[4] Dr. Baars, who once served as a consultant at a treatment center for alcoholism, wrote that "the majority of chronic alcoholics are unaffirmed people."[5] "Unaffirmed," which I will define in more detail below, is another way of describing a person whose inner core is not firm and who feels disconnected, first of all from his or her real self. It is also another way of describing the "shame-based" person spoken of by Carnes, Bradshaw, Kaufman, and many others.[6]

Unaffirmed people cannot "grow up" until their core is made firm through the gift of affirming, unconditional love. Thus, it does not seem to us helpful to call their underlying condition a character defect or wrong, as Bill W. did when he identified immaturity and dependency as fundamental character defects. Unaffirmed people did not make themselves so. No human being chooses to feel insecure and inferior. In my case, at least, I felt profound shame over my condition. Some of my *behaviors* were character defects or wrongs (such as tardiness, social withdrawal, and dishonesty in asking for attention). However, when I judged myself as immature and dependent, this judging of my *basic state* as a character defect only reinforced my feelings of shame. The way out for me was to recognize that my wrongs were my best attempt, as an unaffirmed person, to deal with the pain of not belonging. I believe that lack of affirmation causes "wrongs" ranging all the way from my own tardiness to alcohol abuse to murder.[7] Therefore, in this chapter I want to admit the nature of my *life* and how my hurts have been healed and my losses restored through the belonging that comes from affirming love.

Affirmation Can Save Our Life

Before I speak about my own life, I want to begin with a true story of affirming love. Although Tom worked in a mental hospital, he had no professional training in psychiatry. As an aide, he cleaned the rooms and brought the meal trays. The sickest person in that hospital, a psychotic woman, had been there for eighteen years. Since she arrived, she had never spoken to anyone nor looked anyone in the eye. All day long she sat in a rocking chair and rocked, back and forth, with her head down. The doctors had tried everything they knew to help her, without success.

Tom noticed this woman. He found another rocking chair and pulled it over next to hers. That evening during his meal break he brought his dinner, sat in the chair and rocked beside the woman as he ate. He returned the next evening and the next. He asked for special permission to come in on his days off. He came every evening for six months, rocking beside the woman. She never responded. Finally, one evening as Tom was getting up to leave, the woman looked him right in the eye and said, "Good night, Tom." After that, she began to get well. Tom still came each evening and rocked beside her. Eventually she recovered completely and was released from the hospital.

Tom knew little about psychiatry, but he knew a lot about love. He understood affirmation in its truest sense, something that I received very little of in childhood and found only later.

My mother was like the woman in the rocking chair, except my mother could talk and she did. She screamed nearly all the time. I have only one memory of her speaking calmly and gently to me. When my mother screamed at me, she often said, "You are a bad girl and I am going to break your will!" My mother behaved in this way because she was mentally ill. Her symptoms included an inability to feel empathy. Empathy allows a healthy parent to enter a child's world and sense that the child's needs are different from the parent's needs. Empathy allowed Tom to enter the world of that psychotic woman and gain her trust. Besides empathy my mother also lacked a capacity for healthy guilt or remorse, which alerts us to our unloving behaviors and motivates us to stop. Although my father was capable of both empathy and healthy guilt, he was very limited in his ability to affirm his children. He returned from World War II with post-traumatic stress disorder, from which he never recovered. He was regressed emotionally and in desperate need of affirmation himself. Thus I never received the affirmation I needed from either of my parents.

What Is Affirmation?

By "affirmation," I mean something very specific. Many books in the self-help sections of the bookstores use this word. Sometimes it sounds like a quick-fix technique, something we "do" to others or to ourselves. We may hear someone spoken of as "an affirming person," because he or she frequently compliments others. Although compliments can be an expression of affirmation, they are not its essence. Affirmation is not something that we *do* but something that we *are*. It is a way of being present.

The root of the word "affirmation" is "firm." In the language of St. Paul, affirmation means to help the "hidden self" of another "grow strong" or firm, through the quality of our presence (Eph. 3:16). Tom did not do things for the psychotic woman. Rather, he was present to her in a way that helped her hidden self to grow strong. He rocked when she rocked, communicating to her, "You are good, your world is good and I want to be with you in your world. You belong to me." Tom's presence literally fed that woman life.

We have quoted Robert Bly, who says a boy receives food when he stands in the shadow of his father.[8] This is also true of girls and mothers. My mother's presence did not feed me, and I grew up starving. People everywhere are starving, and not just for physical food. They are starving, as I was, for emotional food. In his study of human attachment, psychiatrist John Bowlby concluded, "the young child's hunger for his mother's love is as great as his hunger for food."[9]

The most common hurt that we have seen in every country where we have given retreats is the lack of affirmation in childhood. In other words, many people have never had their goodness revealed to them by another person who loves them unconditionally. We cannot affirm ourselves, in the fundamental sense that I am speaking of here.[b] We can open ourselves to receive affirmation and we can build upon what we receive, but first it is a gift that we receive from others.

We cannot become our true selves until another person affirms us. We become what others see in us. We become our true selves when we see our goodness reflected back to us in the eyes of another person who loves us. I waited a long time for this, always with the sense that I was waiting to be born.

In his book *Born Only Once*, Conrad Baars describes what I was waiting for. He says that we all have been born once, physi-

---

b) Many self-help and recovery books encourage self-affirmation, for example by repeating positive sayings to oneself, e.g., "I am a lovable person." Such methods can be helpful, as a way of healing habits of speaking to ourselves negatively. By the age of fifteen, most of us received 15,000 to 25,000 negative messages, which led us to develop a habit of negative self-talk. It takes 15,000 to 25,000 positive messages to neutralize the negative ones, and another 15,000 to 25,000 to develop a habit of positive self-talk.[10] However, we question those who encourage recovering people to affirm themselves without also stressing the need to be affirmed by others. We believe that methods of self-affirmation lead to a healthy capacity to maintain a positive sense of self-worth only when 1) we are building upon the affirmation we have been given by others, lest we reinforce the fears so common to unaffirmed and codependent people that we do not have the right to depend upon others and that we must give (to ourselves and to others) what we do not have, and 2) we really believe (at least to some extent) the positive things we are telling ourselves, lest we repress or lie to ourselves about how we really feel toward ourselves.[11]

cally. Many of us, however, have never been born psychically because no one has sufficiently affirmed us. We have been born only once and we are still waiting for our second, psychic birth, our birth as our true selves. Dr. Baars describes how this happens:

> I affirm another when I recognize that he is good, worthwhile and lovable precisely the way he is—period, without the usual addition of "in spite of his shortcomings," since that implies that my recognition and feeling of his goodness is conditional and that he must *do* something. And it is in and through the process of my being aware of, and my feeling of, his goodness that I disclose the other to himself: *"You are good the way you are; this is the way you may be; there is nobody like you; you are unique!"*
>
> I do not add, as is so often done, "I want to help you to become better," since that focuses on his not yet being better and creates in him a sense of being expected to do something in order to be better. The feeling that one is expected to do something stifles the opportunity for growing at one's own pace and in one's own way. . . .
>
> It is in this process of affirmation, this process of *knowing and feeling, without doing,* that I give the other to himself. I do not give him his physical existence as a human being. I give him his psychic existence as this specific unique human being. [12]

The opposite of affirmation is denial. Abuse is an extreme form of denial. No human interaction is neutral; we always either contribute to others' psychic birth through affirmation or we deny them. [13]

Affirmation and Psychic Birth

The critical time for this psychic birth is around age two, when the child first experiences itself as a separate person.

Codependency can begin here, if that separation process is frustrated. Ideally the child should have become tightly bonded, securely attached to its parents in infancy. This secure connection is the foundation for establishing a separate sense of self. We cannot separate from others unless we are sure we are securely connected to them.

Then, around age two, the child needs to be affirmed in its goodness as a separate self. Otherwise, it will become filled with shame. This is not the healthy shame which reminds us that we are human, fallible and in need of God. Rather, it is "toxic" shame, a core sense of being fundamentally flawed and defective.[14] A child who is filled with toxic shame will not be born as its true self and will not be centered in its own identity. As an adult it will look outside for direction rather than trusting what is within.

The small child at this stage is in a terrible dilemma. It has to assert itself as a separate person, in a world of adults who are so much bigger, know so much more and have all the power over that child's life. The child is totally dependent upon these people for survival, and yet it must look up at them and say, "No." Two-year-olds *have to* say, "No." What else can they do? How else, with their limited communication skills, can they say, "I am not you. I am me. I have my own reality, different from yours."

Imagine how much courage you had in your efforts to become yourself by saying "No" to the people whose love and care you most desperately needed. We speak of children at this stage as "brats" and "terrible two's." So they sometimes appear. I am learning to see them as brave little conscientious objectors, who only rarely find someone who understands their situation.

Our friend Jacque told us how she came to understand the dilemma of a small child. Three-year-old Joshua was one of her preschool students. Joshua's parents and older brother were always telling him what to do. Joshua, at least in the eyes of his family, was an uncontrollable brat. The more they told him what to do, the worse he became. So, they sent him to preschool.

Joshua wanted to go, and felt excited about his first day at preschool. It was winter and he arrived all bundled up in his winter coat. He marched down the stairs to Jacque's classroom with his back straight and a radiant smile on his face, looking very proud of himself. Jacque greeted Joshua at the classroom door and said, "Joshua, go over to the coat rack and hang up your coat." Joshua's shoulders sagged and the smile faded from his face. He hung his head and begin to shake it back and forth, silently saying, "No."

As Jacque watched Joshua, she suddenly understood him. She knew he was saying to her, "I cannot do what you ask. I cannot let you be one more person who controls me." Jacque knew he really could not, and she knew how to help him. She got her coat and put it over her arms. She bent her elbows, held them up and began to move her arms like a bird flapping its wings. She said, "Joshua, let's be birds! Do you want to be a bird with me and fly over and land on the coat rack?" Joshua looked up at Jacque and the smile returned to his face, a smile of pure gratitude that said, "You saved me. You got me out of it. Thank you." Then Joshua "flew" over to the coat rack with Jacque and hung up his coat.

Jacque gave Joshua a way out that saved him from toxic shame. On the one hand, Joshua would have felt shame if Jacque had forced him to give in and do what she wanted on her terms, thus denying him any way to assert his own identity. On the other hand, Joshua would also have felt shame if he had resisted what Jacque wanted and been backed into a corner of being a "brat" one more time. He then would have experienced his effort to assert his identity as bad, leaving him disconnected from Jacque and alone. Jacque helped Joshua avoid either of these experiences of shame. She knew how to enter his world. The child's world is the world of play. By entering Joshua's world, she helped him find a way that he could cooperate with her, but on his terms. He could belong to himself and still belong to her.

For the rest of the year, Joshua was the most cooperative child in Jacque's class. Now and then he would put his little arms around her leg, look up and say, "I love you so much." Jacque knew how to connect with Joshua and she knew how to let him be a separate person.

My mother did not know how to connect or to separate. She did not know how to feed me with her presence when I was an infant. Then when I tried to find myself as a separate person (very shakily, since I had little foundation), the only way she knew to handle the awkward efforts of a two-year-old to assert herself was to try to crush them. Because my emotional needs were not met, I not only experienced their frustration, but I also felt shame about having needs. I interpreted my mother's harsh response to them as meaning that my needs, especially needs for love, were bad and that I was bad for having them.[c] The two most powerful tools for the development of self-esteem are the ability to ask for what we want, and the ability to receive what we want.[16] I could not do either one very well. For example, I could not ask directly for attention from teachers.

Affirmation and Psychotherapy

Thus, for many years I felt ashamed, frightened, lonely, insecure . . . as if I belonged nowhere and to no one. I tried to

---

c) This is an example of induced or carried shame, in which an adult who is abusing or neglecting a child transfers his or her unowned shame to the child. My mother was out of touch with her shame over her inability to nurture a child. Thus she "shame-lessly" verbally abused me when I needed nurture from her. I took in from her the shame which she did not own in herself, and developed a "need-shame bind" in which I felt shame whenever I felt needy.[15] See also pages 124–125, for carried shame as a result of sexual abuse.

find healing through counseling. Most of it did not help. I understood why when I read Dr. Anna Terruwe's account of an experience that revolutionized her own counseling practice. She had been trained in a method of traditional psychoanalysis in which the therapist remains emotionally distant from the client, an exaggerated form of "clinical distance." After several months of treatment, one of her clients had not improved at all. Finally, she said to Dr. Terruwe, "Doctor, nothing that you say has any effect upon me. For six months I have been sitting here waiting for you to take me to your heart. You have been blind to my needs." Dr. Terruwe realized that this client "needed only one thing . . . to be treated in a tender, motherly fashion."[17] That is what I needed: to be treated in a tender, motherly (or fatherly) fashion, to be taken to another's heart—to feel that I belonged to someone I could trust.

That is what I was looking for in counseling and rarely found. In saying this, I do not want to convey disrespect for psychotherapy. The three of us are trained in pastoral counseling, and we frequently work collaboratively with psychiatrists and psychotherapists. However, ultimately it is love that heals. Studies of the various methods of psychotherapy have found that the most important element in its effectiveness is not the method used but rather the degree of rapport between therapist and client, i.e., how loved the client feels by the therapist.[18] Although Dr. William Silkworth was not a psychiatrist but a neurologist, Bill W. chose him as his therapist because of his capacity to see the good in alcoholics, so much so that he was known as "The Little Doctor Who Loved Drunks."[19]

Sometimes counseling not only was not helpful, but actually harmed me. These were times when counselors told me I *should* affirm myself, that I was an adult and I *should not* still be in need of parental love, or (from Christian counselors) that I *should* rely on God alone. I believe we look for parental love in those areas where we have not yet received enough of it. Twelve

Step programs recognize this and have a natural mechanism for giving and receiving the affirming, parental love that I needed, through sponsorship. According to Pia Mellody, "the most important characteristic of a good codependence sponsor is someone who can parent and nurture you."[20] When we receive what we really need, we can then parent ourselves and no longer look for parenting from others.[21]

Those counselors who harmed me were probably unaffirmed people themselves, who could not give what they did not have. Perhaps, like myself, they felt ashamed of their own dependency needs. If they had been able to acknowledge this to me, they would not have harmed me. When someone tells me I should not need what I need, the shame over my own needs that I learned in childhood is simply reinforced.[22] On the other hand, I feel respected when someone tells me they cannot give me what I need because of their own limitations.

For the first part of my life, I desperately needed to receive affirmation from other people who could give it. Even now, when I feel substantially healed and rarely empty or afraid, I still need affirming love as a regular part of my life. I've come to recognize an environment of affirming love vs. an environment of denial (the opposite of affirmation), just as I know the difference between fresh air and poison gas. I know that I can't live for very long breathing poison gas. I don't think anyone can. The psychic food of human beings is love. We are meant to live in a flow of giving and receiving this love that literally creates us as human beings. Perhaps that is why A.A. had to have *two* founders, Bill W. and Dr. Bob. Because all 12 Step programs base themselves upon that flow of giving and receiving love that tells us we belong, it takes at least two people to make the process work.

In *Born Only Once*, Conrad Baars speaks of a movement of four parts by which we enter a realm of affirming living where we give and receive the kind of loving presence that heals.[23] When I read his book, I recognized immediately that Dr. Baars was describing exactly what I had always needed. What follows is at once a reflection upon how each part of the movement of affirmation eventually gave me a sense of belonging, and a description of the only way I now know to be a healing presence for others. Although the movement described here is separated into four parts, they are not like the discrete "steps" of a ladder. Rather, they are like four instruments whose music plays back and forth into one melody. We could title the melody "Belonging," since the four parts of affirmation are what make up the experience we are using that word to describe.

BELONGING THROUGH THE
FOUR PARTS OF AFFIRMATION

1. *Knowing Our Goodness*

We can affirm others only to the extent that we have received affirmation ourselves and know our own goodness. Throughout my life there were certain people whose presence was for me like food. These people, who gave me a sense of belonging, were all people who knew their own goodness.

For example, as a child I spent the summers at my grandparents' vacation home at the ocean. In the evenings my grandmother took me walking with her along the beach. She was a healthy person who liked herself. When I walked beside her I could feel her inner strength and her sense of dignity. I felt safe with such a person. Through my hand in hers, I took in the way she was connected to her real self. In those moments I felt connected to my real self. I belonged to myself because I belonged to her. I think those hours with my grandmother kept me alive as a child. Two or three weeks after arriving each summer, I would notice a difference in myself. I was a reflective child, and I remember being five or six years old and thinking to myself, "I am undergoing a personality change. At my parents' home I cannot talk to anyone and I have no friends. Here, all the other children like me."

In high school, my psychology teacher was unusually popular and won many local and national teaching awards. The basis of her giftedness was that she saw every student as good and deserving of the same respect she had for herself. In her presence, I felt respect for myself. She invited me to return to her classroom every afternoon after school and help her wash the blackboards and close the windows. She knew I needed the few extra minutes in her presence. She sensed my interest in theology and during those after-school times she gave me extra books to read by her favorite theologians. I liked the books. But even more I liked the feeling they gave me that I belonged to her in a special way.

In graduate school, my Old Testament professor had that same quality of presence that came from being connected to his real self. I knew that he loved and respected me. I often studied alone in the archaeology library across the hall from his office, where he did research. I would touch the books and absorb the quality of his relationship to them and his sense of belonging to the generations of scholars who had written them. Even when he was not physically present to me as my grandmother or high school teacher had been, I felt affirmed and strengthened by his spirit.

My grandmother, my psychology teacher and my Old Testament professor are examples of how my recovery came in part from learning who could feed me and who could not. I learned not to be fooled by titles and external appearances. What matters most is whether people are connected to their real selves and know their goodness. I have learned from 12 Step groups that sometimes the most wounded, messiest-looking people are the most healing, if they have learned to be real.

If we have studied psychology or gone to a support group, we have probably heard how important it is to know our goodness. But this can still be difficult to grasp, sometimes because of mistaken teaching about humility. I have been helped by St. Thomas Aquinas, who said that humility presumes greatness.[24] In other words, human beings are great. The reason we need humility is to keep our greatness or goodness in perspective, lest we think we are better than God or other people. But if we were not good, we would not need humility.

Tom, the aide in the mental hospital, must have had a sense of his goodness. How else could he give to an unresponsive psychotic woman for months on end, without doubting himself and giving up? Jacque must have a sense of her goodness. How else could she hear Joshua's cry for help, without reacting to his "bratty" behavior and imposing her authority in a shaming way?

2. Noticing Goodness

The second part of the movement of affirmation which creates belonging is to notice goodness wherever we find it. As we notice goodness, it notices us and reflects back to us our own goodness. We can begin anywhere, because the same presence of God fills all created things. If I can notice the goodness in a tree or in a stone, I am more open to the goodness in others and in myself. Thus, reconnecting with the universe helps me belong to myself, others and God.

When I was a child living with a disturbed mother, I went for walks in the woods. Often I noticed a leaf, a blade of grass or a bug and I felt grasped by its beauty. I would sit and look at it for a long time, noticing how utterly good it was. The blade of grass or bug became somehow transparent, like a window through which I sensed a presence. Sometimes there came a moment when something shifted. Then I sensed that presence looking back at me and I felt connected inside. It seemed that presence was noticing how good I was and trying to tell me that I was loved, that I belonged.

Many people who, like myself, had deprived childhoods have a special love for animals or plants. Perhaps it is because it was through these things that God could best tell us we were loved, since the people around us could not convey that message very well.

I became a Christian through my habit of seeing goodness in created things. I come from a Jewish family. I did not know many Christians until I went to college and studied in the religion department. I noticed that many of my classmates had that same presence around them that I had sensed in blades of grass and bugs. When Christian students were together, that presence was especially thick. Eventually I realized that the presence I had been responding to all my life had a name. Its name was Jesus. My capacity to recognize that presence has grown so that now I find it in all people, whether or not they call themselves Christians.

Once I had decided to call myself a Christian, I became a Roman Catholic because Catholicism (at its healthiest), like Judaism, loves the created world. St. Thomas Aquinas perceived "the warmth of the wonder of created things" and believed that every created thing is luminous with the presence of God and is *actively*, almost consciously, trying to reveal God to us.[25]

I believe every created thing is a way God is trying to tell me that I am loved. Thus, in our home, we try to have things that are real—pottery, glass and wood rather than plastic. I have my grandmother's wooden rolling pin and her glass citrus juicer. Sometimes I just look at them or touch them and take in the way they carry her life energy to me. At home we eat only whole foods and I have become sensitive to when a food is still alive and when it has been processed until it is dead. As I prepare whole foods, I touch them as much as possible. I feel their life coming into me even before I eat them.[26]

Somehow early in life I had a sensitivity to the presence of God in all things, and it is one way I took in healing love. Now I try to live that way consciously. People sometimes tell me that I always see good in them. I hope this is true. If it is, I think it is because I learned first to see goodness in leaves, blades of grass and bugs.

3. Being Moved by Goodness

When someone does notice our goodness or when we notice it in another, the third part of the movement of affirming love that creates belonging is to be moved by that goodness—to feel joy and delight in it, without seeking to possess, use or change the other. An image of this is the look on the faces of healthy parents with a new baby, of pure delight that this child exists. I think we all long to have someone look at us in this way. We need to know that our existence makes another person happy; nothing we do, just that we exist.

However, we cannot convey spontaneous delight in one another unless we can feel all our emotions. Our emotions are connected, and if we repress one the others will not function properly either. If we have repressed our grief, we will tend not to feel spontaneous joy and delight. If we have repressed our anger and hate, we will tend not to feel spontaneous love. In this we disagree with Bill W., who discouraged recovering alcoholics from feeling angry. For example, he described anger as "that occasional luxury of more balanced people," which "ought to be left to those better qualified to handle it."[27] We wonder if Bill's distrust of anger contributed to his eleven-year depression, since a common cause of depression is repressed anger.

We can never really know what went on inside of Bill W., but we do know that people who have experienced trauma and abuse in childhood, as he and I both did, usually have repressed their feelings. We could not safely feel them because we lacked anyone mature enough to receive our feelings and help us process them. Without access to a full range of feelings, we cannot live in a flow of giving and receiving love and cannot feel delighted by the goodness of others. I couldn't. I felt depressed most of the time for many years. I had to learn slowly to trust all my feelings and to know that anger, hatred, sadness and despair are as good friends of mine as love and joy. Every one of my feelings has something important to say to me, often way beyond what my head can figure out.

For example, when Denny and I first considered the possibility of marriage, my head said it was impossible. We had lived happily in a celibate friendship for six years, travelling most of the time with Matt. Our ministry together was very successful, but when I thought of continuing to live as we were, I felt sad. I kept pushing away the sadness and refusing to listen to it. The more I did this, the harder it was for me to feel anything, especially joy.

That summer, we were travelling in Canada with Denny's parents. One evening we stayed in a motel that had beautiful wooden chairs. I was standing next to one of the chairs, with my hand on the back. I realized that for several minutes I had been rubbing the wood with my fingers. I knew I was about to cry. I went outside and I did begin to cry, really hard. I was crying out all my repressed sadness. I finally listened to my sadness and it told me that I needed to see the same chair from one day to the next. I needed to care for it and for the people who would sit in it. I needed a home and a family.

During the two-year discernment process that followed, I could not decide for Denny what he should do. But whenever I prayed about what I should do, I remembered the chair. I knew what my sadness was telling me through my fingers about the direction I needed to go in my life to feel joy and delight in myself and in other people.

As I become more friendly with all of my emotions, my capacity to be moved by the goodness of others grows. The more I am delighted by the goodness around me, the more of it I notice—and the more I sense it noticing me and reflecting back to me my own goodness.

4. Revealing Our Delight in Another's Goodness

The last step in the movement of affirming love that creates belonging is to let our delight in another's goodness show, especially in nonverbal ways, and to experience that from others. For example, when I met Denny ten years ago, I was still quite fearful of people, especially men. Denny and Matt were coming to the teaching center that I coordinated, for a videotaping project. On the day they were due to arrive, I tried my usual remedy for self-consciousness with strangers: cooking. I spent the whole day in the kitchen, making the brownies I had heard they liked. Finally the doorbell rang and I went to answer it. Denny stood on the steps for a long time, looking at me and saying nothing. He came inside, and stood there looking at me, still saying nothing. In that stillness, he sensed my fear and awkwardness. He waited until he knew a way to reach me. Suddenly he turned around and fell backwards toward me. Without thinking, I automatically put out my arms to catch him. He stood up, smiled at me, and said with his eyes: "I trust you to catch me when I fall. I am your friend and you are mine. You can trust me when you feel afraid." And I believed him.

Simple things convey to us that we are good and that we are loved, such as the way a friend's face lights up when we enter a room, or the warmth in another's arms in a hug. Studies of human communication have found that 7% of the impact of our communication comes from the content of our words. The other 93% comes from our nonverbal messages (facial expression, tone of voice, body posture, etc.). We can lie with our words, but the look in our eyes and the feeling of our muscles when we hug someone don't lie.[28]

If we have not received enough non-verbal affirmation from others that was believable to us, we can ask for it now. If we were not given loving eye contact as children, we can ask someone we trust to look lovingly into our eyes. If what we said was not received, we can ask someone to nod and smile as we speak. If we were not held and rocked, we can ask someone to do that for us now. [29]

Straightforwardly asking others to care for us in these ways is not codependency. Codependents feel ashamed of their needs and afraid to ask on their own behalf. Thus, they try to get what they need without asking for it (as I did with teachers), or they "give" as a way of getting. This is very different from asking directly for what we need and leaving others free to say "Yes" or "No." Asking for what we need is a healthy way of taking care of ourselves and affirming our right to need other human beings. [30]

So much has been restored in my life by people who were willing and able to give me what I needed in very simple ways. I received the gift of myself by being in the presence of others who saw my goodness and revealed it to me. All of us can help restore in one another the sense of belonging to our true selves by the way we speak to one another, look at one another, hold one another. That is how my hurts are being healed and my losses restored.

We have said that addictive behavior is rooted in shame. The same holds true for the behaviors that go with addictions, what Bill W. called character defects, wrongs and shortcomings. Shame originates when the interpersonal bridges that connect us to others are broken and we are left feeling that we do not belong, even to ourselves. Affirmation restores those broken bridges and creates in us a sense of belonging to our real selves, others, God and the universe.

PRAYER PROCESS

You may wish to get in touch with how you have been given the gift of affirmation. If so,

1. Sit comfortably with your eyes closed and take a moment to grow quiet inside.

2. Recall one moment in your life when you felt nourished and filled by the presence of another person. Maybe he or she was not even paying attention to you. Just being aware of that person made you feel stronger, more connected to your real self. Or maybe that person was attending to you and you recall the way he or she looked at you, touched you, spoke to you or listened to you.

   Perhaps you will think of your parents, your spouse or a favorite teacher. Perhaps you have known little love in your life, and all you can recall is a stranger who smiled at you on the street or a clerk who was kind to you in a store.

3. Imagine yourself there again, and breathe into yourself once more the gift of belonging to yourself that you received in that moment.

4. In whatever way you wish, thank that person and your higher power for the gift they gave you, a part of yourself that can never be taken away from you.

CHAPTER SIX

Steps 4, 5, 6 and 7

HEALING THE HURTS BENEATH WRONGS

Dennis and Sheila think I (Matt) am an expert on these steps. Since an expert has been defined as "an s.o.b. with slides," I don't want to be an expert. Yet my Jesuit tradition has more ways of examining life than A.A. headquarters in New York ever dreamed possible. I have been making an inventory and admitting to God, myself and another human being the exact nature of my wrongs in many ways. These include daily inventories (examens), weekly intimate sharing with other Jesuits or a 12 Step group, monthly spiritual direction, annual eight day retreats, accounts of conscience to my superior and provincial, and especially forty-plus years of going to confession. As a priest, I have heard Fifth Step confessions and thousands of regular confessions. Sometimes I and others have experienced healing. Other times I continued doing the same things I had just confessed. Why don't we always experience healing that removes our "defects of character"? How can the sharing of the inventory in the Fifth Step be more healing? I believe one reason that only 29% of those in A.A. remain sober for more than five years is that the Fifth Step isn't always done in a way that heals the underlying hurts.[1]

Healing the Underlying Hurts

My deepest hurt occurred when I was seven and my brother, John, was two. We thought John had a bad cold. The doctor would not come to our home. We were afraid to take John out in the wintry weather. I kept telling my worried mother that John would be ok. Finally, the neighboring nurse came and told my mother to call an ambulance. John died of a collapsed windpipe five minutes from the hospital. I loved John and I felt responsible. I was sure that my mother would have called for the nurse five minutes earlier if I hadn't told her not to worry. Maybe all the times I wrestled John with headlocks had weakened his windpipe. When my parents told me that God took John to heaven so he could be happier, I remembered all those fights. I thought, "If I had made John happier here, God would not have had to take him away."

I missed the funeral because I was hospitalized with the croup. Instead of grieving John's loss, I swallowed my grief with my Irish mother's words, "He's a saint and happy in heaven." I became a perfectionist who would never make another mistake that would cause someone to die. These reactions are common in children who lose a sibling. Perhaps that is why the psychological handbook DSM-III places the death of a sibling in childhood at level six (with seven being the worst—repeated deaths) and equal to the trauma of repeated physical or sexual abuse. I know John's death changed me from a happy child to a very wounded child.

At age seven I didn't rationally figure out that I could not forgive myself. I only knew I didn't like myself. I began playing with younger children because I didn't have the confidence to play with those my age. I made mistakes when reciting in front of the class and then shameful memories of these mistakes brought even more mistakes. I tried to change this by studying hard. I graduated in the upper 3% of my class and became a champion debater.[a] Yet all this success didn't change my dislike for myself nor my compulsive patterns of acting it out. I kept confessing the same sins year after year.

At age eighteen I joined the Jesuits to become a priest, the most "perfect" calling (I thought). As Dennis mentioned, Jesuit life began with a thirty day retreat and a general confession. Because I could see so much wrong with myself, I typed ten single-spaced pages covering all the sins of my life. Joe Sheehan, my novice-master, looked at the pages and said, "I won't be able to read all this. Just tell me the most important things." I began with what was on the list but found myself saying something I had not written: "I also blame myself for my brother John's death." I broke out into tears and could not continue. Finally I had brought to the light my area of deepest shame, a secret I had kept even from myself. Joe put his arms around me and said, "God loves you more than ever and I do too." At that moment I knew I was loved at my worst. I forgave myself for the first time. I wrote in my diary, "I feel like a cement tomb has cracked open and I am finally free."

From that moment on, I *was* free. I was free even to grieve. My grandmother's death released yet more tears for John. Grieving made a space in my heart for fellow novices who began restoring the loss of my brother John as they now became

---

a) John Bradshaw suggests that "defects of character" are really learning deficits. In my case, I overdeveloped my analytic abilities in order to survive. This overdevelopment was at the expense of underdeveloping my capacity to perceive the world without immediately analyzing and judging it. One symptom of this, which might be called a character defect, is that I tend to be critical and impatient, debating others rather than receiving what they have to say. I find it helpful to see this as a learning deficit that I am filling in as the hurt behind my shame gets healed.[2]

friends and "brothers" to me. As novices, we had two hours of
daily prayer. As I reconnected with God who had loved me at
my worst, I could forgive God more deeply for what I considered God's worst: the moment God took (I thought) my brother
John. I felt reconnected with the universe in our rural, lakeside
novitiate, as I planted trees deep into the nourishing earth. I was
coming alive because I could grieve and forgive the hurt. Even
my perfectionism diminished. For instance, I no longer studied
just to get good grades. I could enjoy literature for its own sake.
Once I stopped blaming myself, I could again reconnect with
God, myself, others and the universe in order to restore my
losses.

Why Wasn't I Healed Sooner?

Why did I get healed by this confession and not by others? I
believe it was because I confessed not just my "wrongs" but also
where I was most hurt. Wrongdoing arises out of hurts. For years
I fruitlessly confessed the same patterns of sin: skipping my daily
prayer, lust, and impatient hostility that debated to put another
down. After I faced and healed the hurt of John's death, these
diminished. Less and less did I angrily avoid God in prayer, lust
for friendship to replace John, or put another down to prop up my
wounded self-image. When a festering hurt heals, patterns of
wrongdoing heal.

Why wasn't the hurt of John's death healed sooner? Hurts
heal to the degree we share the depth of our pain and take in love.
As a child I had papered over my pain with "John's a saint and
happy in heaven. It could have been worse. Dennis or myself
could have died of croup too. Be strong and don't cry." I couldn't
face the pain because I wasn't ready. I wasn't ready because, even

though I come from a loving family, I didn't have all that I needed until I went to the novitiate. There, I felt secure: called to be a Jesuit and loved by nature with its fall leaves reflecting in the placid blue waters of Parley Lake, safe from the hectic pace of the city. Most of all, as I already mentioned, now I had ninety new brothers who could help restore the brotherly love I had lost. Because of this environment of love in which my losses could be restored, I could in my general confession finally let myself feel and be loved in the pain I had hidden most—my shameful failure that didn't prevent John's death and even (I thought) caused it.

Any hurt involves a loss that needs to be grieved with all our feelings and finally restored with love, as indicated in our Reflections on Steps 6 and 7. Under the hurt of John's death were many losses: loss of a brother, of making friends for fear I would lose them like John, of freedom to make mistakes, and the deepest— loss of ability to love myself. When I could grieve this deepest loss where I was most stuck in shame, I could take in life-giving love to heal the hurt. This is not unique to me but the natural grieving process that restores us to life and heals addictions.[3]

Dr. Elisabeth Kübler-Ross discovered that dying persons move through the grieving process toward acceptance of death if they can share with another all they feel about their losses.[4] She found that a dying person goes through five stages: denial (I'll be ok), anger (It's their fault), bargaining (If . . . changes, I will . . .), depression (It's my fault), and acceptance (I'm ready). These same five stages of the grief process are necessary for completely forgiving any deep hurt.[5] Since in the anger stage we say, "It's their fault" and in the depression stage we say, "It's my fault," forgiveness of others and oneself is integral to grieving a hurt so it heals. The following chart shows the parallels for grieving and forgiving a hurt or loss.

FIVE STAGES		
STAGES	IN DYING	IN HEALING A HURT OR LOSS
Denial	I don't ever admit I will die.	I don't ever admit my hurt or loss.
Anger	I blame others for my impending death.	I blame others for the hurt or loss.
Bargaining	I set up conditions to be fulfilled before I am ready to die.	I set up conditions before the hurt or loss can be grieved or forgiven.
Depression	I blame myself for letting my impending death destroy me.	I blame myself for the hurt or loss.
Acceptance	I look forward to dying.	I look forward to growth from the hurt or loss.

We do not move in a straight line from one stage to the next, but back and forth dealing with whatever emotion surfaces next. It is essential to face all our emotions of anger and depression, both to work through grieving a loss and to forgive. A friend who has counseled the grieving for over thirty years told me, "When a person is stuck in grief, the key is to help that person share the stuck anger that is blaming another or the depression that is blaming oneself."

How did I go through these stages? When John died, I denied it by making John a saint, thinking, "It could be worse," swallowing tears so as to be strong, etc. When I did let myself feel the loss, I angrily blamed slow ambulance drivers, my parents for not knowing what to do and God who didn't give John five more minutes to reach the hospital. It was easy to forgive my grieving parents because I could see their tears for John. I only partially forgave God. With passive-aggressive anger I avoided daily prayer especially when God wasn't "good" to me. I bargained with God: "If you are good to me and others, I will trust your goodness and partially forgive you for taking John." Finally, I turned the blame against myself in the depression stage. I blamed myself for telling my mother not to call a nurse, weakening John's windpipe by wrestling, angering God (I thought) by not caring enough for John, etc. I could not heal the hurt because I was stuck in blaming myself.

In my general confession I finally shared not just my wrongdoing but its underlying hurt with my painful feelings of shame and self-hatred. Because Joe Sheehan's love embraced me in my shame, I could forgive myself. I could finally grieve and accept my greatest loss, the loss of being able to love and respect myself. Then I could let love restore my other losses.

Healed Hurts Yield New Gifts

When love heals hurts, then that love transforms patterns of wrongdoing into gifts. Nearly all my gifts have come from the hurt of John's death. The gifts developed from my attempts to have my losses restored. For example, after losing John, I decided that I would never take my other brother for granted or have unresolved quarrels between us. That led to my close relationship with Dennis that makes us want to write this book together and work closely giving retreats. Another gift in my life is my sister, Mary, whom we adopted because we wanted to love another child in our family as we loved John.

As a priest, I enjoy being with people in confession and with those who have lost a child. I know how God healed me and how God can heal them. I have co-authored ten books on healing of hurts. They deal primarily with grieving, the way I myself experienced so much healing. Besides the content, even my gift for writing came from the hurt of John's death. Because I felt so insecure, I wrote out carefully whatever I had to say and soon became adept at writing. I developed almost every gift I now have in order to cope with John's death.

How Did Bill W. Feel About Healing Hurts?

Some feel that this approach of healing the hurts behind the wrongdoing is incompatible with Steps 4 and 5. Since Step 5 focuses on admitting "the exact nature of *our wrongs*," "keep it simple" to them has often meant ignoring the hurts done to us. Yet I believe that Bill W. would approve of my confession that included my hurt. He taught that if the inventory were to heal, it had to include deep emotional hurts that fueled the wrongs.

> Damaging emotional conflicts persist below the level of consciousness, very deep, sometimes quite forgotten. Therefore, we should try hard to recall and review these past events which originally induced these conflicts and which continue to give our emotions violent twists, thus discoloring our personalities and altering our lives for the worse.[6]

Bill saw forgiving the hurts from others as not an addition to the Fifth Step but its natural outcome if we have accepted forgiveness for our own wrongdoing.

Our moral inventory had persuaded us that all-round forgiveness was desirable, but it was only when we resolutely tackled
Step Five that we inwardly knew we'd be able to receive
forgiveness and give it, too.[7]

A Healing Model for the Inventory

My experience of healing the hurt of John's death, and my
experience as a priest of hearing Fifth Step confessions and thousands of regular confessions, have taught me that my inventory or
confession is life-giving if I do three things. First, I ask, "For what
am I *grateful?*" The more I am gratefully aware of my growth, the
more I can encourage it and discover the areas of wrongdoing that
stifle this growth. In Chapter Five Sheila shared the importance
of appreciating our goodness so that it can grow. Secondly, I ask,
"What are the areas of *wrongdoing* for which I need forgiveness
and healing?" These are not just actions but also attitudes that
lead to hurting another or myself. Thirdly, I ask, "Who has *hurt
me*, and can I begin to grieve and forgive this loss?" This locates
the hurt that fuels my wrongdoing and begins the process of
healing it. Bill W. promises this healing.

Once we have taken this step, withholding nothing, we are
delighted. . . . We can be alone at perfect peace and ease.
Our fears fall from us. . . . The feeling that the drink problem has disappeared will often come strongly.[8]

All this can begin to happen by simply taking a moment to
answer the three questions I have found healing.

1) For what in my life am I grateful?
2) For what areas of wrongdoing do I need forgiveness and healing?

3) Who has hurt me and what did I lose? Can I begin to grieve
this loss and receive healing for this hurt?[b]

---

b) An important part of healing hurts, especially in cases of abuse, is
feeling our anger at those who hurt us (the anger stage of the five stages discussed
earlier on pages 111–113). When we are motivated by shame, as is typical of
abuse victims, we may be tempted to bypass this stage and prematurely forgive
the person who hurt us. See the following chapter.

CHAPTER SEVEN

Steps 8 and 9

8. Made a list of all persons we had harmed, and became willing to make amends to them all.

9. Made direct amends to such people wherever possible, except when to do so would injure them or others.

REFLECTIONS

8. *In addition to a willingness to make amends to others, I made a list of all the ways my inner child has been hurt and became willing to make amends to that child.*

9. *In addition to being willing to make amends to others, I made direct amends to that child wherever possible.*

MAKING AMENDS TO OURSELVES

As a Swedish chemist, Alfred Nobel amassed a fortune inventing dynamite and other explosives ideal for weapons. When his brother died, a newspaper accidentally printed Alfred's obituary. Alfred read it and realized that the world would remember him for making a fortune by enabling us to reach new levels of mass destruction. He decided to make amends before he died. Shortly afterwards he used his fortune to found the Nobel Prize, including the Peace Prize which encourages creative efforts to end war and violence. [1]

This process of recognizing that we have hurt another, admitting it and making amends to that person is what steps 8 and 9 are about. When I (Sheila) first studied these two steps, I had two reactions. My first reaction was how wise they are. If we have hurt others, we will never be at peace until we have done what we can to make amends to them, as Alfred Nobel did. My second reaction was the feeling that something is missing. What if I am the one who needs the amends? This idea was not developed in the original A.A. literature. If it had been, perhaps these steps would have included something like our reflections on them:

8. In addition to being willing to make amends to others, I made a list of all the ways my inner child has been hurt and became willing to make amends to that child.
9. In addition to making amends to others, I made direct amends to that child whenever possible.

This is important to me because I find it much harder to make amends to myself than to another person. I always tend to blame myself.

For example, when my mother died in 1985, I inherited her wedding ring. When Denny and I decided to get married I asked a jeweler to recast it to go with the engagement ring Denny had given me. The jeweler was far from our home, so we arranged for them to send us the ring when they had finished. What arrived was not at all what we wanted. It was large and (to me) gaudy looking, and did not go with the engagement ring. We sent it back and asked the jeweler to redo it. The second version arrived two days before our wedding and this one was even worse. It was so big that it made me feel like a glitzy movie star. Not only did I feel embarrassed, but the ring actually hurt. The recast stones, which circled the ring, kept digging into the sides of my fingers.

So, the day after the wedding we returned it once more. From then on, I noticed that every time the phone rang, I was afraid the jeweler was calling to yell at me for bothering her again. I was acting as if it were my fault that she had not made the ring correctly.

Finally she did call to tell me they were ready to mail the ring. She spoke to me in a very loving way, and apologized for not having made the ring as I wanted it the first or second time. I realized what I had been doing. We had hired her, we were paying for her work, she had made a mistake . . . and I was acting as if I needed to make amends to her.

Years ago, I would not even have sent that ring back. I would have taken the consequences of another's mistake and worn something for the rest of my life that I did not like. So, even asking the jeweler to redo the ring was a step toward making amends to myself for all the times in the past when I took the consequences of other people's mistakes. Realizing how I had been blaming myself for the jeweler's mistake, I tried to make further amends to myself by appreciating the way I had held out for what I really wanted. I do that again each time I look at my ring and let myself enjoy how it feels exactly right for me.

Making Amends to Oneself for Abuse

My tendency to make amends for others' mistakes instead of asking them to make amends to me came in part from growing up in a culture where women are taught to take abuse. The abuse I experienced in my home as a child reinforced what my culture taught me, and vice versa. I experienced not only emotional abuse from my mother, but also sexual abuse from a man known to my family. Like most abused children, I blamed myself.

The sexual abuse happened when I was between the ages of eight and ten. I never told anyone about it for a long time. Many people who have been sexually abused have never told anyone in their whole life. The title of a book on sexual abuse expresses well its dark, secretive quality: *Conspiracy of Silence.*[2] This quality is one reason that sexual abuse is so damaging. What can't be shared can't be healed. The gift of the 12 Step groups for survivors of abuse is that they are safe places where dark secrets can be shared.

Sexual abuse is a very common experience, for which many people need to have amends made to their inner child. Estimates of overt sexual abuse of children in the general population range from twenty to more than fifty percent,[3] and sexual abuse is known to be especially common in alcoholic families.[4] These estimates are probably conservative, since they rely on *reported* cases and since they usually do not include the more subtle and covert forms of sexual abuse. Recently we attended one of the programs that Jack McGinnis gives for people in 12 Step recovery. In my sharing group of seventeen men and women, fifteen of the seventeen had been sexually abused as children. Jack tells us that this is typical of the groups who attend his programs. When we visited the California State Prison for women, we learned that almost 100% of the 15,000 inmates are alcohol and/or drug addicts, and that underneath the addiction in almost every case is sexual abuse. The addiction is a way of covering or narcotizing the pain of the abuse. Many treatment centers recognize this and often place women in sexual trauma units before treating them for addiction.[5]

Sexual abuse includes not only overt physical abuse. Covert sexual abuse can be at least as confusing to a child as overt abuse. Covert abuse can occur whenever a parent (or other adult caretaker) asks a child to fill the emotional needs that should be met by a spouse.[6] Other common forms of sexual abuse include: not being given accurate information about sexuality; being given information about sexuality that we aren't ready for, as when a small child turns on the television and sees people exploiting one another sexually; being forced into stereotyped roles of what men and women are supposed to be like; being told that God is masculine only and not equally feminine; advertising that gives us the message that we are sexual objects rather than persons.

Speaking in very general, simplistic terms, victims of sexual abuse, especially overt physical abuse, react in two basic ways: by acting out or by withdrawing. To use Pia Mellody's concept of boundaries, people who act out in response to sexual abuse have a damaged or nonexistent sexual boundary.[7] They cannot appropriately limit what kind of sexual energy comes in and goes out from them. Ninety percent of prostitutes and 83% of people in prison for violent sexual crimes were sexually abused as children.[8] Eighty to ninety percent of mothers in treatment centers for child abuse were victims of incest.[9] In Patrick Carnes' study of recovering sex addicts, he found that 81% were sexually abused as children and 97% were emotionally abused. Carnes recognizes that the actual figures may be even higher, since many addicts don't even get in touch with their own abuse memories until the third year of recovery.[10] Alice Miller insists that *all* abusers were themselves victims of abuse.[11]

My Symptoms of Sexual Abuse

While some abuse victims act out, others withdraw. That is what I did. Instead of a healthy sexual boundary, I had a wall. I withdrew completely from relationships with boys and as an adolescent I never dated. I was terrified in the presence of males. I felt a knot in my abdomen that I imagined as something like the reel of a fishing rod. It seemed to have wires that extended down my legs, out my arms and into my vocal cords. If a man came near me, I felt as if someone had turned the reel so that the wires went tight, keeping me from speaking or moving naturally.

I dressed as unattractively as possible, in shapeless clothes.

Unconsciously, I was trying to hide that I was a woman. (Others find different ways to hide, e.g., sexual abuse victims are an average of twenty-eight lbs. overweight.[12]) I felt chronic sadness. I now know this was grief for the loss of the woman I was supposed to grow up to be. I thought my feminine identity had been taken from me forever.

I felt guilty, as if the abuse were my fault. In my experience, this is a universal symptom among abuse victims, even though a child who is abused is never at fault. It may sometimes appear as if children are encouraging sexual attention from adults. For example, a friend has an adopted daughter whose birth mother was a prostitute. At age three, this child began undressing in front of adult men. She was imitating her mother, who had taught her that the only way to get attention is to behave seductively. Older children normally test out their developing sexuality with their opposite-sex parent, assuming that this parent is "safe" to practice on. The child wants to be affirmed in its developing femininity or masculinity. He or she does *not* want the parent to respond in a sexually inappropriate manner.[13] Sexual abuse victims need to hear over and over that they did not cause the abuse. I like the way Pia Mellody puts it: if you encounter a therapist who suggests you were in any way to blame for the abuse you experienced as a child, *run* from that person. He or she is abusing you too.[14]

Despite all of this, I and other abuse victims think, "It was something I said . . . It was something I was wearing . . . It was something I did . . . It was just *me.*" That is what it comes down to in the end: there was something about the very core of me, about my nature as a woman or as a man, that caused this to happen.[a] The tendency to blame oneself for sexual abuse because

---

a) This is an experience of carried shame, in which the victim picks up and carries the disowned shame of the abuser. Sexual abusers are profoundly shame-based people, almost always as a result of their own unhealed abuse. Pia Mellody describes what happens:

of one's fundamental identity can then easily generalize to all life. *Whatever* happens, I think it's my fault. That's what I thought.

This self-blame for sexual abuse by an older man also affected my ability to take in fatherly love from other men and from the fatherly side of God. When I was in the presence of older men or aware of God the Father, I felt shame over my needs for fathering because I thought they had provoked an inappropriate sexual response. Thus, not only was I betrayed by a father figure, but I was also cut off from the opportunity to learn to trust again through the fatherly love of other men and of God.

Electrical circuit theory provides a helpful analogy. Alternating electric current passed through a coil will induce current in a second coil in close proximity to the first coil. In a similar way, intense feelings surging through an abusive caregiver induce the same feelings in the nearby child victim and become a core of feeling reality. This process seems to happen especially with the feeling of shame, but it also happens with anger, fear and pain. . . . Later, as adults, these abuse survivors have recurrences of the same feelings they absorbed in childhood but they do not know them as such; instead, the feelings appear to manifest themselves as overwhelming reactions to present-day events. . . . The principle is this: Whenever a major caregiver is abusing a child while *denying* or *being irresponsible with* his or her feeling reality, the feeling reality is very likely to be induced in the child who becomes overwhelmed by the caregiver's feeling reality. . . . children's internal boundary systems are not fully developed and they cannot keep from taking on the feelings of the adult offender. . . .

Shame is the primary feeling passed to the child. I believe this because it is "shameless" to abuse a defenseless child. A shameless person is one who is denying his or her own shame, which passes directly to the child.[15]

See also page 94.

Healing Sexual Abuse and Making Amends to Myself

The healing I finally found came largely through healing prayer to Jesus and through relationships with healthy people. Jesus is my higher power. I am comfortable bringing my inner child to him in prayer, but I think God could have used many other ways of healing me.[b]

Some friends prayed with me several times over a period of about six months, using the "Prayer of Creative Imagination." In this type of prayer, we get in touch with a painful memory, re-enter that scene in our imagination, invite Jesus to join us there, and then watch what Jesus says and does. As these friends prayed with me, I went back in my imagination to the experiences of abuse and invited Jesus to come and join me.

In the prayer session I remember most clearly, Jesus entered the room and intervened to stop what was happening. He was obviously very angry that I was being hurt. He picked me up and held me until the fear I was feeling left. Jesus then put me in the arms of his mother, Mary, who stood in the corner of the room. He went over to the man who had been abusing me and put his hand on the man's shoulder. As he did so, Jesus looked at me and

---

b) Even though I experienced Jesus as healing me, the people who mediated his healing were an important part of the process, since they were channeling into me not only God's love but also their own level of psychosexual integration (or lack of it). The healing prayer experience described here was a positive one. However, I had another, extremely negative and destructive experience of people praying with me who were not in an authentic, growthful relationship with their own sexuality. The issue is not that a person must be perfectly healed in this area in order to help others. The issue is honesty and a willingness to grow. I have learned, for example, to respect recovering sex addicts as having great power to heal in this area, because they have learned to be honest. See Patrick Carnes, *Don't Call It Love, op. cit.*, 383–390, for his witness to how those who have been most wounded in their sexuality can become the teachers of sexual health to our culture.

silently communicated that this was a very wounded man for whom he had compassion.

Looking back with all that I have learned since then, I see how Jesus was making amends to my abused inner child. First, just by entering the situation Jesus let me know I wasn't alone anymore. The secret could be shared. Jesus then intervened to stop the abuse in a powerful way. I no longer felt like a helpless victim with no one to protect me.

When Jesus became angry on my behalf, I knew he really cared about me. A person who loves us does not remain silent and "objective" if we are being hurt. Also, when Jesus was angry on my behalf he gave me permission to be angry on my own behalf. He validated my anger, anger that I had turned in upon myself and that had become that pervasive pattern of self-blame and of taking responsibility for other people's mistakes.[c] Alice Miller writes that recovery from any kind of child abuse requires an "enlightened witness," another person who recognizes the abuse for what it is, stands unreservedly on the side of the child, and validates the child's feelings. Jesus and the people praying with me were my enlightened witnesses.[17] I have so often found in working with other sexual abuse victims that this experience of an enlightened witness (Jesus or another person who loves us) is the turning point in healing.

---

c) In becoming angry on my behalf, Jesus was helping me to hold others accountable for abusing me rather than blaming myself. This does not mean I was now blaming others. Accountability and blame are not the same. Holding others accountable means telling the truth about who did what and owning my feelings about what they did. Blame means I judge others as intrinsically "bad" because of what they did. The difference between blame and accountability is often misunderstood. More traditional A.A. people sometimes perceive ACOA and Coda groups as encouraging blame, when in fact such groups (if they are healthy) encourage accountability. Bill W. did not seem to understand the difference between blame and accountability, and in his writings he seems so wary of blaming others that instead he encourages blaming oneself. He wrote,

Jesus then held me for a while to fill in the love that I needed, and took me over to his mother Mary so that she too could hold me. I feel comfortable relating to Mary in prayer. However, I think her importance was not that she is Jesus' mother but rather that she is a feminine figure whom I trust. For another woman, God might use a beloved grandmother, aunt or female friend. I needed to relate to a feminine figure as a way of experiencing reconciliation with my own femininity, which I had blamed for the abuse. I also needed reconciliation with my mother, whom I blamed for not protecting me. Girls tend to see their mothers as the guardians of their femininity. When a girl's femininity is violated, she wonders, "Where was my mother?" Sometimes, mothers know when their daughters are being abused, especially within the family. I do not mean to blame mothers. I suspect these are often women who were abused themselves and who were never protected or taught to protect themselves. They then grew up to marry abusers and now do not know how to protect their daughters. Moreover, to face the painful reality of their daughters' abuse would require such mothers to face the repressed pain of their own abuse.[18] Other times, the mother really doesn't know her daughter is being abused. In either case, I have often noticed a need for reconciliation with the feminine, and that is what Mary did for me. A male sexual abuse victim may need something similar from a trusted model of masculinity.

Finally, when Jesus communicated his compassion for the man who had abused me, he helped me to have compassion too and eventually to forgive. It was important that I forgave, not only to free the man, but also to free myself from resentment. However, it is equally important that this came at the end, after I had really honored and respected my anger and knew that my wounded inner child was the one who needed the amends. Our

---

for example, ". . . every time we are disturbed, no matter what the cause, there is something wrong *with us*. If somebody hurts us and we are sore, we are in the wrong also."[16] In this, we disagree with Bill.

anger at abuse is our dignity, the voice of our own integrity saying, "You may not do this to me." I do not think we have the right to forgive another until we have honored this voice within ourselves, however long that takes. When we do honor it, our forgiveness comes from our real self and is authentic.[19]

When I really grasped that I was not to blame for the abuse that happened to me, and when I saw that Jesus was angry on my behalf and wanted to make amends to me, then I began to make amends to myself. I began caring for the little girl inside myself whose feminine identity had been so wounded.

In prayer, I imagined going home with Jesus as an eight- or ten-year-old child and asked Jesus' parents, Joseph and Mary, to care for me in all the ways they cared for Jesus. I asked them to let me be around their healthy love for each other as a man and a woman. In my everyday life, I did something similar. I stayed near people whose sexuality felt wholesome and responsible to me, and avoided people who I sensed were exploiting one another. I stayed away from anything that felt scary or uncomfortable, such as movies with sick sex in them—even if other people laughed at me for it. If someone told a dirty joke that made me feel demeaned as a woman, I left the room or (when I could gather enough courage) told them I didn't like it. I bought clothes that fit me and made me feel feminine. In all these ways I made amends to myself for having believed that my femininity was bad.

Over a period of about six months, as I received healing prayer and as I cared for myself, my fear of men diminished. One day that knot of iron in my abdomen dissolved. It has never returned. I began to enjoy being a woman. My tendency to self-blame also diminished greatly. I still struggle with it, but now I recognize it much more quickly for what it is and I can usually work my way through it. I keep recovering as I continue making amends to myself. Every time I talk or write about sexual abuse, I feel as if I am caring for all women (and men) who have been sexually abused. It's another way of making amends to myself.

Much of my recovery now comes from marriage to a healthy man like Denny (who was my best friend for eight years before I married him) and friendship with Matt, neither of whom treats women as sexual objects.

Making Amends to Others

My tendency always to blame myself came from sexual abuse and also from the way my mother, instead of looking at herself, always accused others (including me). When my mother told me I was a bad girl, I believed her. In a sense, I am the opposite of my mother. She always blamed others and I always blamed myself. I almost died of blaming myself too much. My mother did die of blaming others too much.

In June, 1985, a group of friends joined us in celebrating a healing Mass for my mother and all her ancestors. We prayed especially for healing of any ways in which my mother's brain damage had been passed down through her family line. Six months later, in December, my mother died suddenly of a heart attack. We learned that she had been seeing a social worker, Wally, during the year before she died. I had not seen her during that time, so we invited Wally over to share with us what her last year had been like.

Wally told us that when he first met my mother, he did not like her. He thought she was an obnoxious, antisocial person. Then, six months before she died (around June) she changed. She started to show kindness and concern for other people. Wally began to like her. My mother, who had never before shown any evidence of a conscience, began saying things like, "I have really good children. Why was I always so mean to them? I love my husband. Why did I treat him so badly?" My mother was getting in touch with genuine guilt and remorse, with her need to make amends to others. Never having experienced this before, she didn't know what to do with it. She didn't know that guilt has a remedy, which is to apologize and receive forgiveness.

Wally speculated that the pressure of a lifetime of uncared for guilt built up inside my mother's heart. Combined with her chronic high blood pressure, it caused the heart attack that killed her. Wally also said that my mother died happier than ever before in her life, because she had a real relationship with herself for the first time. She was getting in touch with the truth of her life. She was coming home inside and she belonged to herself. Thus she also could belong to someone else. Wally was her first real friend.

Amends and Shame

Making amends heals shame. Although my mother and I handled it very differently, each of us suffered from a profound core of shame. We each felt alienated from our real self. Shame arises when the bond between two people, the "interpersonal bridge," is broken. This happens whenever I treat another as less than or more than myself. Shame is healed when the interpersonal bridge is restored.[20] Restoring the bridge means restoring the equality and the sense of common humanity between us, since we cannot really have a relationship with someone whom we perceive as less than or more than ourselves. The real purpose of amends is to restore our awareness of our common humanity. Because I have usually tended to see myself as less than others, making amends to myself is also my best way of making amends to others. I restore my sense of having a self that is equal and capable of being in relationship with them. On the other hand, my mother protected her core of shame by seeing herself as better than others. For her, making amends to others would also have been her best way of making amends to herself. By admitting her share of fault, she would have given herself the gift of a common humanity that could enter into real relationship. Although my mother did not know how to make amends, even her awareness that she needed to do so was enough to make her capable of friendship with Wally.

Making Amends Is a Matter of Life and Death

A desire to make amends to others whom we have hurt is built into us. It's a matter of life and death that we act on it. When Alfred Nobel found a way to make amends, he could die in peace. When my mother didn't know amends were possible, it killed her. At those times when I really am at fault, if I don't make amends a part of me will die. This is the wisdom of Steps 8 and 9 as they were originally written.

When we looked at these steps with Jack and talked about how unbalanced they seemed to us, he agreed. But he added, "Many people who come to A.A. have been drinking for twenty years. They've destroyed everyone around them. They've cheated and robbed and raped and killed, and they're loaded with guilt. They *have* to make amends to others to relieve that guilt." The dimension we want to add is that sometimes the person who has been destroyed, cheated, robbed, raped and killed is ourselves— and then we *have* to make amends to ourselves.

GIVING AND RECEIVING AMENDS

Sheila focused on making amends to ourselves. I (Dennis) will focus on two other aspects of making amends: making amends to another and asking another to make amends to us. I will do this by sharing two stories about a part of myself I call "Peace at Any Price." Although the beet story and playing airplane with my dad (Chapter Three) was my first memory of Peace at Any Price, I also met him in a dream.

I dreamed that I was hurriedly riding my bicycle to the

airport. I knew I would be late for my airplane. So I was relieved when I spotted a yellow taxi parked in front of a house. I rang the doorbell, and a woman holding a faceless, blob-like child answered the door. I said, "I need a cab driver to help me catch my plane." The woman responded, "The driver will be right with you." She closed the door. But no driver came. So I rang the doorbell again. When the woman answered the door, I asked, "Well, where is the cab driver?" Pointing to the faceless blob in her arms she said, "He is your cab driver." That blob-like child and the airplane reminded me of how I sometimes felt as a child, such as when my dad and I played airplane while eating beets. At those times, and any other time a caregiver made it harder for me to trust my own thoughts and feelings, my personhood disappeared and I felt like a faceless blob.

Since that dream I have spent a lot of time with that blob-like child I now call "Peace at Any Price." That child is the part of me that avoids conflict. The dream made me aware that if I am going to catch a plane or get where I am going in life, then one of my main tasks now is helping my inner child, Peace at Any Price, grow up. One of the ways I have seen that child grow most is through amends. Thus Steps 8 and 9 have become an important part of my life.

Making Amends to Another

My first story is of making amends to another. Years ago, I lived in Omaha's inner city. So did many transients. They always seemed to want more than I could give them. I wanted them to go to A.A. or somewhere else to get help. They said such programs had never helped them. They wanted food. If I gave them food, then they wanted money and a ride too. No matter what I did, they always left angry and disappointed. Eventually I found a way to avoid any further conflict. When I saw one coming, I crossed the street. I thought to myself, "Maybe this crossing streets isn't such a bad thing to do. I have nothing in common with them. I'm optimistic; transients are depressed. I work (though Sheila and Matt might dispute that); transients don't work." Then I asked myself, "What do I dislike most about them?" I knew the answer immediately. "They dropped out of life, gave up."

When I said, "They dropped out of life," I realized that what I disliked most about transients was also what I disliked most about Peace at Any Price. Transients often had dropped out of life to avoid any further conflict. Likewise, to avoid any further conflict with the transients, Peace at Any Price had dropped out by crossing the street. What I hated most about the transients and myself was that we both compulsively avoided conflict by dropping out. I needed to make amends to the transients for my arrogance and self-righteousness that had scapegoated them.

The next day I baked some cookies. I invited the transients to eat cookies with me on the front steps. They began to share their stories about why they dropped out. Hearing their life struggles made it easy for me to apologize for judging them so harshly. I also shared with them Peace at Any Price's story, what he feared about them, and how he didn't want to be crossing so many streets anymore.

As I reconnected with the transients through cookies and stories, I felt as if I were reconnecting with Peace at Any Price, too. As the transients shared their stories, I recalled more about how Peace at Any Price developed within me. I grew up across from a public school. Our pastor, Fr. Daly, taught us that there was little chance of salvation outside the Roman Catholic Church. He said that it was a temptation to be around Protestant public school kids or anyone else who might contradict what I was taught. Even as a first grader, I wanted to avoid any such conflict. So, instead of cutting across the public school playground, which would have been the most direct route to my parochial school, I started crossing a lot of extra streets. Thus Peace at Any Price started practicing even back in first grade how to feel self-righteous and how to avoid conflict by dropping out and crossing streets. As the transients and I sat together on the front steps, I could see that little first grader dressed in a sailor suit and blue tennis shoes joining us. His welcoming smile grew as he ate cookies and listened to the transients' stories. Often when I am making amends to a transient or to another, I am making amends at the same time to my inner child.

Asking Another to Make Amends to Me

The second story deals with asking someone to make amends to me. Two years ago, after a long discernment process, I decided to marry Sheila. I had lived with other Roman Catholic priests who married and experienced rejection from some in our church. I feared a similar reaction. So, I thought of telling only a few people and having a small wedding. Although avoiding such conflict would make Peace at Any Price happy, it would have left me isolated at the time when we most needed friends. What helped me change my mind and decide to celebrate a wedding with all our friends was knowing that I would have Sheila's help in facing any conflict. Often such an added sense of belonging or walking with another calls me out of my addictive Peace at Any Price behavior.

As a way of connecting with our friends during the two months before our wedding, Sheila and I wrote about 500 personal letters. In each letter we explained our discernment process and said how much we wanted them to continue journeying with us. The trouble with writing 500 people was that more than 500 responded back. Our mail began arriving in TV-sized cartons. When the first carton of mail arrived, I looked at the return addresses and sorted the letters into two piles. One pile was for people I knew would respond respectfully. The other was for those whose response I feared. Sheila and I began by opening the letters from those we feared the most. The third letter we opened was from Joan (not her real name). For over fifteen years, Joan and her husband had been good friends who had often reached out to me in caring ways. Her letter contained everything I feared. For seven pages Joan said that neither she nor her community wanted anything to do with me. Since as a priest I had decided to marry, I had obviously given my life over to the "lusts of the flesh and the devil."

Sheila and I had promised each other that we would write back to everyone who wrote to us. In our reply to Joan, we said three things. First, we thanked her for caring enough to write back. Second, she could disagree with us. We wanted to remain her friends anyway. Third, if she wanted us to explain our decision more thoroughly, so that she could understand it better, we would be happy to do that.

When I reread my letter, I felt so sad and exhausted that I decided not to mail it. Two days later when I read my letter to a friend, I knew what was wrong. I sat down and rewrote it, again saying three things. The first was exactly the same: we appreciate your care in writing back. The second and third were: "When we read your letter we felt sad and angry, like someone thrown into jail without a trial. We want to continue to be your friends, but to do this, we need you to walk in our shoes and write back to us what you discover as you do so." In short, we were inviting Joan to make amends to us by walking in our shoes.

When I mailed that letter, the sadness lifted and I felt energized. Weeks later I realized that since writing back to Joan, I had stopped putting the incoming mail into two piles. That is because I no longer felt my former fear. I discovered that what I feared most was not what people would say, but that I would sell myself out. I sell myself out whenever I fear conflict so much that I become a compulsive people pleaser. That's when Peace at Any

Price, instead of insisting that people respect him, gets exhausted trying to explain himself so that everyone will be pleased. I sometimes imagine Peace at Any Price passed out over a typewriter from the exhaustion of writing endless explanations.

By inviting Joan to make amends, I was making amends to Peace at Any Price for every time I have thought, "I need to please everyone, no matter what." I felt as if I were standing behind Peace at Any Price at the typewriter, giving him a backbone and allowing him to stand straight and grow up. Peace at Any Price is learning that it is OK to think what you think, feel what you feel, and trust what you trust.

As Sheila mentioned, whenever we make amends, we restore the interpersonal bridge. My self-righteousness with the transients had damaged that bridge by making me feel "one up." Joan's self-righteousness with me had also damaged the bridge as I felt "one down," like someone thrown into jail without a trial. But through amends, I can eat cookies and share my story with the transients, and I can invite Joan to walk in my shoes. Such amends restore the interpersonal bridge, a sense of the common humanity between us. This gives a sense of belonging to our inner child and releases its genius. The genius of Peace at Any Price is relational. When given a sense of belonging, the focus of his relational genius changes from "how can I have the fewest enemies" to "how can I be the best friend." This transformation happened, for example, when I knew Sheila would face with me any conflict coming from the outside. Thus instead of telling only a few friends about our marriage, I could risk writing personal letters to 500 people. In such moments of belonging, Peace at Any Price receives a backbone and a new name, "Builder of Lasting Friendships." This transformation of Peace at Any Price into Builder of Lasting Friendships continues in each moment of amends. Whether I eat cookies and share stories with the transients or open the letter of apology that Joan eventually sent us, new doors for lasting friendships open. Through a lifetime of

amends and moments of belonging, Builder of Lasting Friendships' genius matures. It is because of the gradual maturing of this
genius that by the time of our wedding we had 500 friends to
write to, all but eleven of whom still choose to continue building
a lasting friendship with us.

Whether we are talking about Peace at Any Price, or an
addiction to alcohol, sex, etc., such addictions are not primarily
about peace, alcohol, or sex. Rather, every addiction is about a
dying inner child. As in the case of the beet story and Peace at
Any Price, addiction begins when the child deep within receives
the fatal message, "don't trust, don't think, don't feel . . . don't
be." Unless we make a place in our heart where our own dying
inner child can recuperate, we can't take into our heart the dying
and hurting children we meet each day on the streets. As Alice
Miller writes,

> . . . the repression of our suffering destroys our empathy for
> the suffering of others. . . . If I as a helpless child was abused
> and *am not allowed to see this*, I will abuse other helpless
> creatures without realizing what I am doing."[21]

In an addictive person or an addictive country, what always
loses is the child. Perhaps that is why in our country, the mortal-
ity rate for a child born in Detroit is higher than for a child born
in Afghanistan.[22]

Maybe our society is not that different from the one Jesus
was born into under King Herod. Herod was addicted to power.
He ordered a massacre of the children. The child Jesus had to
flee. That fleeing child probably had the same question as Peace
at Any Price when responding to Joan's letter, or as Sheila's
abused little girl: "How come they don't want me?" What we lose
in addiction is our child. That is why we stress in our reflections
on Steps 8 and 9 "making amends to our inner child."

In the meditation that follows, you can allow your inner

child to receive amends. Perhaps, as in the case of Sheila bringing her abused child to Jesus' family, you may wish to allow someone else (your higher power, a grandmother, etc.) to care for your child. Or in the case of myself giving cookies on the front steps to Peace at Any Price, you may wish to care for your own child.

MAKING AMENDS TO YOUR INNER CHILD

1. Take some deep breaths as if breathing from the bottom of your toes. Breathe out and bless all the space around you.
2. Place your hand on your heart. Ask your higher power to bring to your heart one thing that you still wish were different about your childhood.
3. Share with your higher power a few of the memories connected with what you wish were different.
4. As you share, be aware of how you still carry those memories in your body. Maybe they feel like a weight on your shoulders, a lump in your throat, a head bent in shame, or an angry fist. Pay attention to each part of your body, how it felt when the incident happened and how it feels now.
5. Imagine a child with those same feelings.
6. Allow that child to be cared for. Like Sheila, you may bring it to Jesus' family. Or you may wish to care for it the way you would one of your children or grandchildren, maybe breast-feeding it or bouncing it on your knees. Perhaps you want to take that child for a walk and show it something special like a leaf or a favorite stone. Allow your child to be cared for without trying to change it or fix it in any way.

HEALING BLOCKS TO AMENDS

Often we keep trying to work one of the 12 Steps but get blocked because we have been hurt and fear being hurt in the same way again. At each step we can heal the blocks coming from negative memories of hurts. We have long recognized that working through negative memories in therapy or grief groups brings new freedom. But freedom also comes from working with positive memories. This is no surprise, since in 12 Step groups members often share their positive memories of victories over their addictions, and find such memories empowering them to live even more freely.[23]

Only recently has psychology discovered the power of positive memories for overcoming addictions and compulsions. For example, a recent study divided participants in a weight loss program into a control group and an experimental group.[24] They watched the same video presentations with one exception. The experimental group's presentation contained the subliminal message, "Mommy and I are one." Subliminal messages are conveyed so quickly that only the unconscious picks them up. This message that triggered positive memories of being one and loved as a child helped the experimental group lose more weight and keep it off. When the same subliminal message was included in a reading program for disturbed adolescents, the reading scores of the group with the subliminal message improved four times more than the control group. Similarly, of those in a program to stop smoking, only 12.5% still refrained from smoking a month later. But of those who had the same program plus the subliminal message, 67% (or more than five times as many) had quit smoking.

Positive Memory of Making Amends

As I (Matt) share my positive memories of making amends, you may recall some of your own. When I was a child and angry at Dennis, I took out my anger by robbing his bank. This habit grew into taking other things. One of my earliest memories is being about four and going to the corner grocery with my dad, Dennis and our red wagon. At the checkout counter where customers stood, the grocer had put candy and other items one would buy on impulse while waiting. At my eye level hung beautiful plastic knives for cutting cheese. Before I knew it, I had the blue one in my pocket. Suddenly, I thought the green was nice too. So I took it and three others. On the way home, I dropped the knives into the grocery sack so they wouldn't fall out of my jacket pocket while pushing the wagon uphill. I figured my mother would unpack the sack and think my dad had bought the knives for her. But my dad unpacked the groceries and saw the knives. "Where did these come from?" he asked. He glanced at my red face and gave me an angry lecture about taking the knives right back and never stealing again.

Fortunately, my mother could see how I was already ashamed and didn't need the lecture. She took the knives in her hands and stroked them. "They really are beautiful. I don't need five knives but I would like to keep one for our picnic basket. Which one do you like best?" I dried my tears and helped her choose my original favorite, the blue one that got me into trouble because it was so beautiful. She agreed with my choice. I felt understood rather than just full of shame. Because she had stood in my shoes and understood me, I could understand her view too. For her I wanted to take the four knives back, pay for the blue one that I kept, and apologize. Mr. Root, the grocer, was grateful I apologized, and he even gave me a cookie for being honest. I felt as though I was seven feet tall, a grown-up who could do the right thing. I also stopped stealing. I felt understood by my mother and no longer had to cover my shame by stealing so Dennis would be less rich than I. When I dread making amends, I recall this incident. It usually empowers me to move past my crippling shame into making amends. Once again I feel as though I stand seven feet tall. Amends mend me.

RELIVING A POSITIVE MOMENT OF AMENDS

1. Recall a positive memory of making amends. (I have many such memories: saying I was sorry after an argument; notifying the bank it put an extra $500 into my account; apologizing for denting the car and my dad replying, "I'm glad you weren't hurt. We can always repair a car.") Or recall a positive memory of amends made to you. (E.g., a friend sent me back a cassette tape he had borrowed years earlier. He enclosed a note: "I am in A.A. and want to make amends for all my wrongdoing so nothing stands in the way of my sobriety.") Relive this memory until its energy to make amends lives inside you. Let it grow until it is powerful enough to overcome any shame.
2. With this energy see if you want to make amends to someone you have hurt.

Negative Memory of Making Amends

Often our body remembers hurts our heads forget. For a long time I didn't like to shake hands with people when introduced to them. It wasn't a fear of intimacy because I was open to giving a hug. Only a handshake felt insincere. One day when focusing on my hand and how it felt insincere, a memory came that fit the insincere feeling. I was four years old and Dennis had started a fight with me. My mother was tired of endlessly sorting out who started it. So she told us to stop fighting and made us say to each other that we were sorry. Then she made us shake hands. I remember squeezing Dennis' hand as hard as I could because I was still angry that he didn't get punished and my righteousness wasn't vindicated. I had to swallow my angry words, "It's not fair! He started it!" To get even, I robbed Dennis' bank. As this memory shared its story, I could feel my hand relax.

The next step was to see what I needed. I needed what I wish had happened (instead of what actually did happen) So, in my imagination I constructed the ideal way that I wish my mother had handled the situation. She comes and listens carefully to my side. She says "I don't know who started it. If Dennis did, you have a good reason to be angry." Then she hugs me. Then she listens to Dennis. She tells him that he too has a good reason to be angry and hugs him. Finally she says, "I don't know who started the fight. You are the best boys in the world so I hate to see you fight and hurt each other. Do you think you two can work it out together?"

Once I knew what I needed, to be understood as a four-year-old, I shared that part of myself in a letter to my higher power, Jesus.

Jesus,

    I hate having to share everything with Dennis. He just took our coloring book. He scribbled on all the best pages with a black crayon. The only ones left are pictures of girls. I don't want to color those. I told him to stop because he didn't ask me which ones I wanted to color. He just took the crayon and scribbled another page and another. I grabbed the book from him to show my mom and he hit me so I hit him back. Then he cried like a cry baby even though I didn't hit him as hard as he hit me. My mom heard him scream and told me I have no business hitting him because he is younger and I ought to know better. I tried to tell her the way it happened.

But she kept saying there are better ways to solve things than hitting a younger brother.

So I have to shake hands again. We each have to say we are sorry. I'm not sorry. I'd hit him again. That's the only way he'll quit hitting me. He's not sorry either. He'll scribble up another coloring book without asking me what ones I want to do. I feel as if no one listens to me. If I'm angry, it's always my fault. Next time he scribbles up our book, I'm really going to hit him. I want to be able to solve this my way rather than shake hands.

Then I listened for what Jesus wanted to say back to me. I sensed him saying:

Matt,

I saw what happened and it was just the way you said. Your mother gets tired of sorting out what happened and just wants peace so she makes you both shake hands. Dennis will scribble up another coloring book. As a two-year-old he is always looking for another way to assert himself. He doesn't listen when you tell him he can't color it. That just makes him want to do it. You should be angry. You have a right to try solving things your way and see if it works rather than always be forced to shake hands.

The next day we had the following conversation:

Jesus,

You seem to understand some but it doesn't sound as though it ever happened to you. You had perfect parents.

Matt,

I know how you feel because it happened to me too. Mary and Joseph were returning to Nazareth by separate routes. Each assumed I was with the other. I stayed behind thinking they would know I was with my cousins. My cousins were going to spend two days shopping so I told them I would be in the temple. It was great asking questions and talking to the teachers. I felt like a grown-up who could stand on his own two feet and solve things.

But my parents came back and were angry that I stayed behind. They didn't ask me why I stayed but just told me how upset they were. They told me it was dangerous to be alone in the temple. I defended myself. Didn't they know that I had to be here? I told them how the teachers invited me back and said they would watch over me because they liked me. It felt good not to back down. I was more grown-up than my parents thought.

Matt, I want to tell you more of how I like the way you stand up for yourself when you get angry, too.

After these conversations with Jesus, I felt my four-year-old no longer angrily wanting to settle the fight. What I wanted in my fantasy to happen with my mother (to be heard and be recognized as big enough to resolve problems) happened with Jesus. That helped me not only to sincerely shake hands but also to be less angry when another didn't hear me. I can calmly say, "When you said that, I didn't feel understood. Let me say again how I see the situation and then would you please feed back to me what you heard?" If I do again get blocked, I ask Jesus or an understanding friend for what I need.

HEALING THE BLOCK TO AMENDS

1. See yourself as a child, when you were blamed for something you didn't do, such as starting a fight. Where are you? What are you wearing? Feeling? Saying? Whoever cared for you comes into the scene. What does this person do and say? How do you feel? (Hurt, misunderstood, put down, ashamed, guilty, fearful, manipulated, etc.?)

2. What do you wish this person had said and done?
3. What you wish had happened (instead of what actually did happen) is what you still may need. State your need in a sentence or two. (E.g. I need to be heard in my anger and understood rather than shake hands.) Share this with your higher power or a friend and ask for what you still need. How does that person respond to you?
4. What could you do now to help fill this need?
5. You may wish to continue with the Guided Journaling process on pages 219–220.

CHAPTER EIGHT

Step 10

10. Continued to take personal inventory and when we were wrong promptly admitted it.

REFLECTION

I continued to remain faithful to a daily process of listening to the ways I am connected to and disconnected from myself, others, the universe and God, and followed my longings to deepen my sense of belonging to all.

TELLING THE TRUTH VS. RELIGIOUS ADDICTION

Step 10 speaks of taking an inventory and promptly admitting wrongs. At first glance, it may sound as if the most important things to acknowledge are our failures. However, Bill W. knew that,

> . . . inventory-taking is not always done in red ink. It's a poor day indeed when we haven't done *something* right. Even when we have tried hard and failed, we may chalk that up as one of the greatest credits of all.[1]

In our Reflection on Step 10, we added a positive perspective:

> I continued to remain faithful to a daily process of listening
> to the ways that I am connected to and disconnected from
> myself, others, the universe and God, and followed my long-
> ings to deepen my sense of belonging to all.

When speaking about this step, I (Sheila) often mention
how important it is for women to see themselves positively, since
our culture teaches us otherwise. Like subordinate classes of people everywhere, women in our culture are generally taught to see
themselves as wrong. Men, on the other hand, as the dominant
class, are generally taught to see themselves as right. Moreover,
men are taught to prove their rightness by competing with others.
Bill W. was a man, writing initially for a fellowship that in its
early years was almost entirely male. (One of the titles originally
suggested for "The Big Book," *Alcoholics Anonymous*, was *One
Hundred Men*. It was rejected because of the objections of Flor-
ence R., at that time the only woman in A.A.)[2] Like many men
who have been raised to dominate and compete with others, Bill
perceived himself and other alcoholics as tempted by the sin of
pride—he called it "alcoholic grandiosity." The antidote was
"ego-deflation," which Bill saw as the purpose of all 12 Steps.[3]
For Bill, Step 10 was a way of daily resisting the temptation to
pride by deflating the ego. Perhaps that is why Step 10 mentions
only wrongs and does not include Bill's recognition that "inventory taking is not always done in red ink." However, Liz, a recovering alcoholic, told us, "I've been going to A.A. meetings for
twenty years and I've never seen a woman walk in who needed to
have her ego deflated. We already feel as though we're nothing."
So often for women, "sin is not pride, the exaltation of self, but a
refusal to claim the self God has given."[4]

   Recently a man pointed out to me that he too finds it difficult to claim his real self and tends to always see himself as
wrong. He made me aware that although in our culture men are
encouraged to "win" and never "back down" or "give in," many

men, too, carry a deep-seated, shameful conviction of being basically wrong. Perhaps, then, the woman who made the following comment on Step 10 was speaking for many men as well as many women:

> Admit that I'm wrong? I say I'm wrong for breathing air. I need to say I'm *right* for a change.

In light of such comments, Charlotte Kasl suggests rewriting this step as follows:

> Continued to trust my reality, and when I was right promptly admitted it and refused to back down. We do not take responsibility for, analyze or cover up the shortcomings of others. [5]

For me, the importance of Step 10 is not to get in touch with being either right or wrong. Instead, this step means getting in touch each day with what is real within me and "trusting my reality." If, as we have suggested, the beginning of all addictions is denial (running away from what is real within us), then the remedy for addictions is telling the truth. In Step 10 I try to tell the truth about who I am for that day. Trusting my reality to me means trusting that I am most in touch with God when I am most authentically in touch with myself.

Trusting the Reality of My Hate

My most powerful experience of this occurred several years ago, while my mother was still alive. My father had ulcerative colitis. When I arrived to visit them, I saw immediately that he was dying. He weighed only 116 lbs. (compared to 180 lbs. a few months before), was so weak he could barely stand, and his hair and fingernails were falling out. I called his doctor and learned that because my mother had not allowed my father to get medical treatment earlier, he now needed surgery to save his life. He was too weak to get himself to the hospital, and I realized that I would have to intervene.

I told my mother that my father was very sick and would die unless we took him to the hospital. She began to scream at me, just as she did when I was a child and asked her for anything. She said, "No! No! Why are you bothering me! You are a bad girl!" In my adult mind I knew hospitalization was reasonable and necessary. Yet I began to feel as I did when I was a child and my mother screamed at me: frightened, confused, guilty and ashamed.

I asked Jesus to help me, and suddenly I experienced something very different. A wave of pure, clear feeling went through me, something like the chill of an ocean wave. I did not recognize the feeling at first, as I had never consciously felt it before. Then I realized it was pure, clear hate. It was one of the most emotionally real, authentic moments of my life.

I did not know what to do with my feeling of hate and I began to question it. In a sense, I was taking an inventory of what was going on inside me and judging it to be wrong. Once again I asked Jesus to help me. I expected him to tell me to forgive my mother more deeply or be more understanding of her. Instead, I heard Jesus say to me,

> Your pure hate is my pure hate.
> Your pure hate is my gift to you to help you say no.
> When you say no, it's me within you saying no.

After that, I no longer felt frightened, confused, guilty or ashamed. I knew exactly what to do, and I felt full of the energy of that hate to help me do it. I went to my father's room, almost literally picked him up and carried him to the car, and drove him to the hospital. He had surgery the next day and recovered completely. The doctors told me that without the surgery he would have died within a few months. He lived five more years, long enough to fly out to our wedding by himself and walk me down the aisle.

Looking back, I know that Jesus and I together were not hating my mother herself. Rather, we were hating the sickness in her that was destroying her real self. But I think it's better that I did not try to figure that out at the time. Instead, I just trusted what was most real within me, the feeling of pure hate, and used its energy.

It may sound strange to speak of Jesus' hate, but if Jesus was fully human as well as fully divine, then he had every part of human nature except sin. (Heb. 4:15) Thus he had every emotion, since every emotion has a special purpose within the human psyche. The purpose of hate is to help us resist evil. I suspect that Jesus often felt pure hate because he was so sensitive to evil, just as he often felt pure love because he was so sensitive to good.

Trusting Our Own Reality vs. Religious Addiction

Besides codependency, the addiction which we see most often in our work and which can be the most difficult to recognize is religious addiction. Religious addiction is hard to recognize because it looks so good from the outside. If the beginning of all addictions is denying what we really feel, then the beginning of religious addiction (for a Christian, anyway) is denying what we really feel and substituting what we think a good Christian *should* feel. Religious addiction is using Jesus (or Mary, the Bible, the Pope, the eucharist, or any other good religious thing) to get away from our own reality. I almost did that. If I had used my ideal image of Jesus, who I thought would never hate anyone, to get away from and lie about the hate I really did feel as I confronted my mother, I would have had the beginning of a religious addiction. Instead, in that moment at least, I was relating to Jesus in a healthy way. I let Jesus be with me in my hate and he helped me to be with it.[6]

Jesus was not a religious addict. He didn't substitute what the priests and pharisees said he *should* feel or think or do for his own reality. Jesus belonged to himself and, I think, he was always honest about what he felt. God as I understand God loves all my pure feelings and wants to use them for my good. That can only happen when I learn to tell the truth, in the sense of recognizing and owning what is real within me. As I try to do this each day, I get better at it. I can identify more accurately the truth of my life for that day.

In her book *Co-Dependence*, Ann Wilson Schaef says that for a recovering codependent, "even the smallest lie can plunge us back into our disease."[7] In other words, distorting the truth of who we are in any way (to please others, to meet our own expectations of who we *should* be or what we *should* feel) is like an alcoholic taking that first drink. Each day I want to get better at telling the truth about what is real within me because I need to do that for my recovery.

As I get better at honoring pure hate or any other authentic inner response to my life experience, I come closer to feeling what Joseph Campbell calls "the rapture of being alive":

> People say that what we're all seeking is a meaning for life. I don't think that's what we're really seeking. I think that what we're seeking is an experience of being alive, so that our life experiences on the purely physical plane will have resonances within our own innermost being and reality, so that we actually feel the rapture of being alive.[8]

REVIEW OF LIFE

I (Matt) get excited about this step because it has given me much life since I entered the Jesuits in 1960. They introduced me to a daily inventory of both the positive and the negative, called the examen or review of life. I have continued it for over thirty years because, of all my spiritual practices, the examen has brought me the most growth. I especially need the examen because of my pessimistic outlook. (In Africa I did manage to find a more pessimistic person. When I told him that we should change our pessimism because optimists live longer, he replied, "It serves them right!") I am also a perfectionist. At a workshop, ten people might compliment me while only one person might tell me something that could be improved I forget the ten compliments and remember only what could be improved. I can take Step 6, "Were *entirely* ready to have God remove *all* these defects of character," and turn it into striving to be perfectly ready to be perfect. So, for me to literally live the Tenth Step by taking an inventory of only my wrongs (instead of focusing on the positive too) would only deepen my perfectionism and pessimism.

Bill W. often did an inventory of only the positive:

> One exercise that I practice is to try for a full inventory of my blessings and then for a right acceptance of the many gifts that are mine—both temporal and spiritual. Here I try to achieve a state of joyful gratitude.[9]

Thus each night my examen or inventory focuses on two questions: For what am I grateful? For what am I not so grateful?[a] When I discover something I am not grateful for, I name it, feel it, and appreciate that I am not denying it and God is with me in

---

a) The gratitude questions are simply one way of discovering the day's consolation and desolation. Any area of growth can be the focus of questions such as the following:
When did I give and receive the most love today? The least?
When was I happiest today? Saddest?
What was the day's high point? Low point?
When did I follow my 12 Step program most? Least?

it. Healing occurs to the degree I accept all my feelings. In this way I honestly acknowledge pain, and I take in experiences of love and happiness. Then I can usually fall asleep with a grateful heart.

Whatever I sleep on enters the unconscious. For example, when I had lost something or didn't know an answer to a problem, often I would wake up the next morning with the solution. Why? Because whatever I am thinking about when falling asleep continues to be processed in my unconscious during the night. If I go to bed grateful and expect to awaken saying "thank you," the gratitude bathes the unconscious and I awaken more grateful. But if I go to bed resentful, I fill the unconscious with more resentment and awaken ready to strike back. Learning this has even changed my dreams. I no longer fall off cliffs headlong into paralysis or death but now bounce back with more life. The longer I sleep with a grateful heart, the more I heal my unconscious. So now when the alarm rings, I can say, "I think I need another hour of healing my unconscious," and fall back asleep without feeling guilty.

The Sioux Way to Wisdom

I learned to appreciate the examen and especially its focus on gratitude while teaching on the Rosebud Sioux Reservation. I taught six subjects, published the school newspaper, ran an education center, and cared for 100 boarders. I existed on five hours of sleep and had no time for the examen that until then I had done daily.

While teaching Lakota, the Sioux language, I visited the Sioux holy men (wicasa wakan) to collect their Lakota stories and wisdom. They had learned how to grow in the lethal reservation environment with 70% unemployment, 70% alcoholism, and a suicide rate ten times the national average. These wicasa wakan had a stream of visitors trying to resolve marriage crises or seeking prayer for some difficulty. People sought them not because they had many experiences (some couldn't read and had not travelled off the reservation) but because they prayerfully reflected on what experience they had. They were men of experience, not experiences. Daily they arose at dawn to listen to the new day. Each year they made a vision quest (hanblecheya) of at least four days' solitude to listen to the Great Spirit and find Wakantanka's road of peace and wisdom. As I taught history, I learned from the historian Arnold Toynbee that those who shaped the great civilizations all had this same trait, regular reflection on their lives.

I often asked a wicasa wakan, "Would you tell me about a hanblecheya that was special for you?" Old Bill Holy Eagle shared a time he was sitting in his sacred space (an area four steps square) on his holy mountain toward evening. The goal of a hanblecheya is to treat everything that enters that sacred space as a brother or sister bringing a message from the Great Spirit. Bill told me:

> I was sitting there praying over and over "mitakuyepi oyasin" [all my relatives] as the eagle soared overhead and the mosquitoes feasted on my naked body. With difficulty I welcomed all the mosquitoes and the cold as my brothers. Then came the greatest challenge. Sintehla [rattlesnake] slowly slithered toward where I was sitting motionlessly with my legs crossed. I was the warmest thing on the mountain. I knew Sintehla would be attracted toward my warm body. He so scared me that his three foot length looked like thirty. Yet I had to welcome him as a brother in my sacred space. So while trembling I kept praying "mitakuyepi oyasin, mitakuyepi oyasin . . . "
>
> Sintehla came right for me and started to crawl in the space under my crossed legs. To keep warm he coiled his body against mine. I wanted to jump ten feet straight up. Yet I knew that if I suddenly moved, this would scare Sintehla

and he would bite me. I began shaking and his tail began rattling. So it was a matter of life or death to stop shaking and to welcome him as my brother. Finally the Great Spirit gave me love for my brother and I said with my heart, "mitakuyepi oyasin." At that moment, as if he had finished his mission, Sintehla quit rattling, uncoiled and left for his home. He had given me power to welcome all as my brother or sister.

With that story Bill gave me some of his power to welcome even a rattlesnake and grow from it. I wanted to be like Bill who could grow from every event because he took time to reflect. I began again to do my examen at the end of each day. To stay awake when I was so tired, I would type it or occasionally share it with a friend. I needed to do something because I was burning out fast and sinking into the negative, depressed atmosphere of the reservation. One day I buried a favorite student who dropped out of school, got drunk, shot his brother, and then killed himself. My depression felt like a rattlesnake that I wanted to run from rather than ask for wisdom. At the end of that day, I remembered Bill and how he welcomed everything as a friend and teacher. Instead of running from my depression, I asked it, "What do you need?" My depression felt dog-tired. Thus I promised it that I would cut back on activity. It also felt desperately alone and longed for someone who had walked through the despair of family murders.

With this longing came the image of a community leader, Pearl Walking Eagle. Pearl had buried four children and her husband, Harvey, whom a drunken neighbor killed. I was at Harvey's funeral where Pearl prayed for the murderer's family who had to be protected by the police from neighbors bent on revenge. Her prayer of forgiveness brought peace to her heart and to the community. I visited Pearl, shared my grief with her, and felt her understanding. My despair lifted, and I even felt inspired to visit another drop-out student. I convinced him to come to my education center to work for his GED graduation certificate so his life wouldn't also end in drinking and an early death. He didn't persevere, but Pearl's hope persevered in my heart so I could now cope with disappointment.

Each night my review of the day would show me what was giving me life (what I was grateful for) and what was draining life from me (what I was not so grateful for). One week I discovered that I received life as I visited families, so I did more of that. A month later I found that visiting was now draining life, so I did less. My depression lifted and I felt more alive than ever because each day I was finding and choosing life. This practice more than any other kept me growing during my seven years on the reservation.

Daily, Weekly, Monthly and Yearly Reviews

Besides a daily review, I review each week and share on Thursday mornings with four other Jesuits in my community. The meeting is optional but we all attend because we catch life from each other's sharing. Before I lived in this community, I did the same with a weekly ACOA or Coda meeting. I also review my month and share it with my spiritual director and confessor. Finally I review and share my year with a group of six Jesuits each summer at a lake. We have been doing this for the last twenty years. Each of us takes half a day to share our year and hear the other's reactions. We do this because we want to be known by one another so well that we can help each other discern new directions. For example, several times Dennis and I shared how giving occasional retreats brought us the most life. After hearing this for several years, the group suggested we spend less time in our jobs (I was teaching the Sioux and Dennis was the superior of a Jesuit community) in order to do more part-time retreat work. When we shared their discernment with our provincial, he told us to take the next fifteen years to do retreat work not just part-time, but full-time.

Often people come to me in spiritual direction or on a retreat thinking I have a crystal ball to discern their future. A generous man will ask if he should give up his job and work for the church full-time. A mother will ask if she should volunteer in the community or spend more time with her children. Another person will ask how to heal depression. These are good questions but impossible for me to answer—except for this answer. I simply tell them to spend the last ten minutes of their day prayerfully answering two questions: "What today gave me life?" and "What took life from me?" If they do this faithfully for a month or two, they will answer their other questions for they will know what changes will bring more life. The will of God is always to give and receive more love and life.

Recovery by Living Fully in the Present Moment

The daily review helps not only to discern the future but to live fully in the present. The list of activities for recovery is daunting: proper diet, exercise, rest, prayer, creative work and hobbies, journaling, reading, support groups, etc. My problem is that I can do these and profit little. For example, one morning I tried to write and couldn't get going. I decided that I was too sleepy and needed a brisk swim to wake up. While swimming I started thinking about lunch and finished my swim quickly because I was hungry for a hamburger. While eating the hamburger, I hurried because I had wasted the whole morning without writing and by now had a pile of mail waiting. When I finally returned home to write, I felt exhausted and still couldn't write despite the swim and good lunch that should have renewed me.

That night during my review of the day, I realized that I had rushed through things to get them done rather than enjoying the present moment while swimming or eating. So when it came time to write in the afternoon, I had even less life than I started with in the morning. The daily reviews help me catch what I am doing because I *should* rather than because I *enjoy* it. Recovery doesn't come with frantically doing more activities but with enjoying and fully living the present activity.

I want to close with a story of how I need the examen to help me find the positive in each day. Last Holy Week I was driving from Minneapolis to Omaha at 2 A.M., trying to get back home for the Good Friday services. I had a rental car that averaged thirty-two miles per gallon on the trip to Minneapolis. So I thought that with the 13.3 gallon tank, I should have more than enough gas for the 367 mile trip home. But just as I approached Omaha, the motor gave a final gasp. I was furious that I had run out of gas five miles from home with a red traffic light in front of me. Then the red light turned green and I kept coasting even though it seemed slightly uphill. I saw an open gas station two blocks ahead. The car made it right up to the premium gas pump and not an inch further. I was angry that my car was still four feet short of the unleaded pump, since I never waste money on premium gas.

During the last five miles home, I did my review of the day. Then it dawned on me that I had driven 362 miles while fighting sleep and arrived at the best pump. Yet I had been focusing negatively only on the five remaining miles and the extra money for premium gas. That is why I need the daily examen. I want to be grateful for the 362 miles and the premium gas that I take for granted.

The Serenity Prayer that opens every 12 Step meeting summarizes the process and results of the daily review of life.

> God, grant me the serenity to accept the things I cannot change, the courage to change the things I can, and the wis-

dom to know the difference. Living one day at a time. Enjoying one moment at a time. Accepting hardship as a way to
peace. Taking, as Jesus did, this sinful world as it is, not as I
would have it. Trusting that you will make all things right if I
surrender to your will so I may be reasonably happy in this life
and supremely happy with you forever in the next. Amen.

PROCESS FOR REVIEW OF LIFE

Perhaps you can tell, after Matt and Sheila's enthusiasm,
that the review of life (examen) is an important part of our day.
Without it, I (Dennis) doubt if we would enjoy traveling and
working together as much as we do. For the past five years, we
have ended most evenings together with an examen process that
has two steps. First, we take about five minutes of quiet while we
each ask ourselves two questions: For what moment today am I
most grateful? For what moment today am I least grateful? Secondly, we share those two moments with each other. Usually the
entire process takes about twenty minutes. When we are very
sleepy, we can easily finish in ten.

I like three things about this process. First, although the
examen is helpful when done alone, we do it together. When I
share with another, not only do the moments I choose to speak
about become more real and important to me, but so do the
people with whom I share. This is why 12 Step groups put so
much emphasis on regular sharing with another, e.g., a sponsor.
In my case, sharing the examen gives Sheila, Matt, and myself a
chance to enter into one another's heart.

We are surprised by how sometimes what for one of us is the
moment of most gratitude, is for another the moment for which
he or she is least grateful. For instance, my favorite country is
Guatemala. My favorite recreation there is bartering in artisan
markets where everything is made by hand with beautiful, rain-
bow colors. One evening, during a trip to Guatemala, I shared

with Sheila and Matt that I was most grateful for being able to buy six handwoven shirts. Because I had bartered the price per shirt down from $12 to $4, I had bought one for myself and five for my friends. That same evening Sheila reported my bartering as her moment of least gratitude. Sheila makes things by hand (she knitted sweaters for everyone in our family), and thus knew that each shirt would take about five days to make. So when the seller said, "$12," rather than me offering $4, Sheila wanted me to say "$24." We returned to Guatemala again last year. This time, before I bartered in the market, I bartered with Sheila about what would be a fair price. At the end of the market day when we did the examen, we all agreed that our moment of most gratitude was the shirt purchase we made in which both the seller and ourselves felt like winners.

The second thing I enjoy about our examen process is that it makes me aware of moments I might easily pass by as insignificant. For instance, one day we were at an English/Spanish conference in the U.S. where the anglos played music in the morning and the hispanics in the afternoon. That evening at examen I shared that I was least grateful for the way the conference had dragged when the anglos played. Then I shared my moment of most gratitude: the hispanic group and how their music revived the conference. On one level, those two moments seemed very insignificant. But as the months went by, we all began to notice a pattern in which often our moments of gratitude centered around hispanic people. We knew that God's will for us is to do, whenever possible, more of whatever gives us the most life or gratitude. So, we decided to study Spanish in Bolivia and spend the following three years giving retreats in Latin America. Insignificant moments when looked at each day become significant because they form a pattern which often points the way to how our higher power wants to give us even more life.

The third thing I like about the examen is that it has helped me appreciate all day long how the voice of God speaks through those moments for which I am not so grateful. I am an optimist, the opposite of Matt. I think that I live in the best of all possible worlds, and Matt is afraid I'm right. My addiction is to always be happy and grateful, and to compulsively deny or escape sadness and pain. But the examen has helped me recognize painful moments as they happen. Now I try to be with my feelings of sadness and pain, and hear how God is speaking through them.

In the last chapter, for example, I shared about the initial letter I wrote replying to Joan's criticism. At first, I thought I had written a good letter. But when I reread it, I recognized feelings of sadness and exhaustion inside me. Feeling all that, I knew that when I would do the examen that evening, my letter would probably be what I was least grateful for. Years ago, before I first started doing the examen, I probably would have reread the letter and, not being in touch with what I was feeling, mailed it. Though the examen began as only a reflective process that I did in the evening, now I discover this process happening almost automatically during my day. So, I didn't mail my initial letter to Joan. Two days later, when I recognized how to rewrite the letter, the sadness finally left. As I rewrote the letter, I discovered exactly what the strangled voice of God inside my sadness wanted to say to me: "Stand up for yourself." If I had mailed the initial letter and not listened to my sadness, the moment I was least grateful for, I probably would have missed what God wanted to tell me. But rather than talk more about how much I enjoy the examen, let's enjoy it together.

EXAMEN OR PERSONAL INVENTORY

1. Put your feet flat on the floor, take a few deep breaths from the bottom of your toes, up through your legs, your abdominal muscles and your chest. Breathe out and bless all the space around you.

2. Place your hand on your heart and ask your higher power to bring to your heart the moment today for which you are most grateful. If you could relive one moment which one would it be? When were you most able to give and receive love today?
3. Share with your higher power exactly what was said and done in that moment that made it so special. Breathe in the gratitude you felt and receive life again from that moment.
4. Ask your higher power to bring to your heart the moment today for which you are least grateful. When were you least able to give and receive love?
5. Share with your higher power what happened in that moment that made it so difficult. Allow your higher power to be with you in whatever you feel without trying to change or fix it in any way.
6. Give thanks that you are an alive, feeling person. If possible, share as much as you wish of these two moments with a friend.

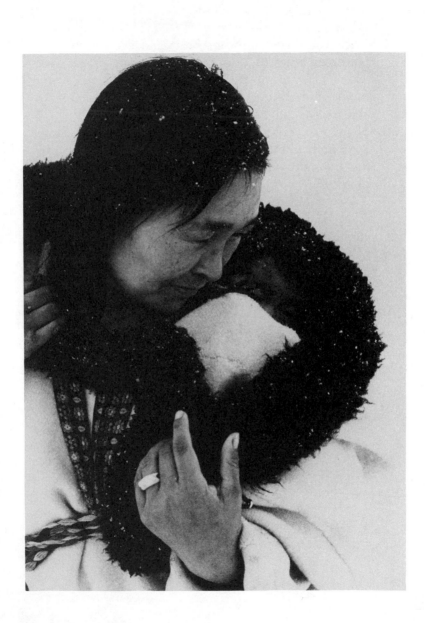

CHAPTER NINE

Step 11

11. Sought through prayer and meditation to improve our conscious contact with God *as we understood God,* praying only for knowledge of God's will for us and the power to carry that out.

REFLECTION

Since I become like the God I adore, I sought through prayer and openness to life to heal my image of God so I could be guided by God's unfolding love.

WE BECOME AS ADDICTED
AS THE GOD WE ADORE

I (Dennis) want to share what has changed me most in the last fifteen years. Although I don't want to stereotype Germans, like many of my German ancestors, I was born a self-righteous German. As an adolescent, self-hatred caused by scrupulosity kept my self-righteousness from manifesting itself. But once healed of my self-hatred through my general confession, I became a "self-righteous addict." I saw the mistakes and errors in everyone but myself.

For example, I have already shared how I crossed the street to avoid transients, thinking myself much better than they. But transients are one thing, your wife is another. In Chapter Four, Sheila mentioned that she used to dislike herself for being overly sensitive to criticism. She wished she could be less easily upset, like me. What she didn't share was that my behavior only added to her distress because I was giving her the message, "What's wrong with you for being so upset?" Everything, I thought, was her problem; I couldn't understand why she wasn't perfect, like me.

For years I admitted to my higher power that I was powerless over my self-righteousness. I made fearless and searching inventories regarding my self-righteousness. I made amends to those like the transients and Sheila whom I hurt. At the same time, I also tried healing prayer. And though the 12 Steps and healing prayers healed me of many things, they did not heal me of my self-righteousness.

Then one day, I noticed that my self-righteousness had greatly diminished. That doesn't mean I no longer saw the mistakes and errors of others. But almost as soon as I did, I usually noticed the same things in myself. Rather than feeling superior to and separated from others, I felt connected with them and with myself. Why, I asked, after so many years of struggle, was there suddenly and almost automatically such a wonderful change in my life?

As soon as I asked the question, I knew the answer. I changed when my image or understanding of God changed. We become like our parents whom from early on we adore, even with all their faults. But we also become like the God or higher power we adore. Unfortunately, the God I adored was German. Being a self-righteous German God, my higher power could see all the mistakes and errors in everyone else from his (at the time I had an all-male God) judgment throne. If he did not like what he saw, he could even separate himself from others by sending them into hell. And if my God or higher power could be a self-righteous German, then no matter how hard I worked the 12 Steps or prayed for healing, I would probably never change because I become like the God I adore.

This is true in every aspect of my life. For instance, since my German God punished those who didn't measure up, I could easily refuse giving the transient, whom I judged didn't try hard enough, the coat or food he obviously needed. I could also refuse Sheila, who seemed "too upset," the time she needed to work things out with me. But when my image of God changed, I also changed. A key to changing addictions and other behaviors is to change our image (or to use Step 11 language "our understanding") of God.

When Bill W.'s Understanding of God Changed, Bill W. Changed Too

Although I was shocked that a change in my image or understanding of God could change me so radically, this would not have shocked Bill W. He also changed when his understanding of God changed. Two moments in Bill's life, his moment of coldest hatred and his moment of deepest belonging, reveal how Bill's understanding of God changed.

Bill's moment of coldest hatred happened one winter night while riding a Brooklyn subway. He noticed a father and mother huddled together with their three children. Bill knew they were riding the subway only because they had no other place which could keep them relatively warm and dry. He saw the mother unbutton her blouse to try to feed a child who was too old for breast feeding. Then he became aware of another passenger, a priest, who also saw the family's dire situation. Bill would never forget the "almost beatific smile that moved across" the priest's face. Catching Bill's eye, the priest said in a cold voice, "Do not worry, God will provide."

Bill stood up and, towering over the priest, shouted, "What

God? And what will he provide?" Furious, Bill declared that he could not believe in a child-abusing God who let innocent children starve.

> The pious shit this man was passing out, asking these decent people to believe, didn't come from any faith, from any caring, and how, he wanted to know, could a God of love, a God who cared, watch innocent children starving? Then, having found himself tricked into using the priest's vocabulary, his fury mounted. He didn't believe in his God, he declared, or in his God's begotten son. They were not facts. Heaven and hell were not facts. He and his church were making people believe through fear, and medieval superstition, and he gestured toward the family, poor, suffering bastards who were afraid not to believe. [1]

When Bill got off the train at the next stop, he realized that he had to search for a God who was not a child abuser. Although Bill rejected a God who was a child abuser, he could not accept a God who was love. When such a God was preached to him, Bill said, "I became irritated and my mind snapped shut against such a theory." [2]

Bill "fought long and hard against the idea of God." [3] Finally, he realized that his alcoholism was terminal. Knowing he had nothing to lose, and having just heard the recovery testimony of his friend Ebby, Bill became willing to open himself to a new experience and understanding of God. He cried out to the God he didn't believe in. And to Bill's surprise,

> I became acutely conscious of a Presence which seemed like a veritable sea of living spirit. . . . "This," I thought, "must be the great reality. The God of the preachers. . . ." For the first time, I felt that I really belonged. I knew that I was loved and could love in return. [4]

When Bill's understanding of God changed from a distant and impersonal God to a God of "belonging," Bill changed too. His sense of belonging in that moment was so strong that Bill "never again doubted the existence of God. He never took another drink."[5]

Writing on Step 11, Bill describes how alcoholics often move through multiple understandings of God, from no felt sense of God, to a God who is indifferent to the needs of human beings, and finally, to a God with whom they can enjoy a deep "sense of belonging." Bill sees Step 11's "sense of *belonging*" as the "greatest reward of meditation and prayer." When this happens Bill concludes, "all will be well with us, here and hereafter."[6]

Thus for Bill, the goal of the 12 Steps is not for a person to stop drinking, but rather to open a person to a spiritual experience like the one that changed Bill. Bill promises that what happened to him will happen to anyone who seriously follows the 12 Steps:

> If we have carefully followed directions, we have begun to sense the flow of His Spirit into us. . . . We have ceased fighting anything or anyone—even alcohol. . . . If tempted we will react sanely and normally, and we will find that this has happened automatically. We will see that our new attitude toward liquor has been given us without any thought or effort on our part. It just comes. That is the miracle of it.[7]

The Twelfth and last step sums up the goal of the Steps as a "spiritual awakening," which, once experienced, the alcoholic carries to other alcoholics.

> Having had a spiritual awakening as the result of these steps, we tried to carry this message to alcoholics, and to practice these principles in all our affairs.

When Our Understanding of God Changes, We Change Automatically

Whether it be Bill W.'s alcoholism or my self-righteousness, the key to most recovery is the same: a spiritual awakening that almost always results in a new understanding or new image of God. How one understands God was so important to Bill W. that *"God as we understood God"* is the only phrase in the 12 Steps or in the 12 Traditions that Bill W. chose to emphasize by underlining.[8] Even though Bill was adamant about the importance of a healthy understanding or image of God, he was just as adamant that alcoholics come to it on their own. Thus A.A. welcomed even atheists and agnostics. Bill hoped that such alcoholics would come to a new understanding of God as they attended A.A. meetings and experienced how belief in a higher power brought wholeness to other alcoholics. But often I and others work the 12 Steps for a long time and yet experience little recovery and, contrary to Bill W.'s hope, little or no change in our understanding or image of God. How does that change finally come about?

I want to share with you how my image of God finally changed. I hope that you will not feel pressured to change your image of your higher power in the same way. Rather I hope that my story will be an occasion for you to ask yourself the question: Is there *any* way that I am being invited to change my image of my higher power?

My image of God changed the day I noticed a woman at one of our retreats crying. I asked her, "Do you want to share what you're feeling?" She told me her name was Hilda. The previous night her son had tried to commit suicide for the fourth time. Then she told me the longest list of big sins I had ever heard. Her son was involved with prostitution, was a drug dealer, and had murdered several people. She ended her list with, "And what bothers me the most is that my son says he wants nothing to do with God." Then she asked me, "What will happen to my son if he commits suicide without repenting, and wanting nothing to do with God?"

At the time I thought God would probably send her son to hell, but I didn't want to tell her that. So, I was glad that my fifteen years of theological training had taught me what to do when I don't know how to answer a difficult theological question: ask the other person what he or she thinks. "Well," Hilda responded, "I think that when you die, you appear before the judgment seat of God. If you have lived a good life, God sends you to heaven. If you have lived a bad life, God sends you to hell." Then, looking me straight in the eye, she concluded, "And since my son has lived such a bad life, if he were to die without repenting, God would certainly send him to hell."

I have to admit that I agreed with Hilda. But I didn't want to say to her, "Hilda, you're right. Your son would probably be sent to hell." Not knowing what to say, I was again grateful to my fifteen years of theological training which taught me a second strategy: when you don't know how to solve a theological problem, then let God solve it. So I said to Hilda, "Close your eyes. Imagine that your son has died with all these big sins and without repenting. Imagine also that you are sitting next to the judgment seat of God, and your son has just arrived there. Squeeze my hand when you can imagine that."

A few moments later Hilda squeezed my hand and she described to me the entire judgment scene. Then I asked her, "How does your son feel inside?" She answered, "My son feels so lonely and empty." So I asked Hilda what she would like to do. She said that she would like to throw her arms around her son. And with her eyes still closed, she lifted her arms. She began to cry as she imagined herself holding her son ever so tightly. Finally, when she had stopped crying, I asked her to look into God's eyes and watch what God wanted to do. God stepped down from the throne and embraced Hilda's son, just as Hilda had done. And the three of them, Hilda, her son and God cried and held one another.

I was stunned. What Hilda taught me in those few minutes is the bottom line of all healthy spirituality: God loves us at least as much as the person who loves us the most. God loves us at least as much as Hilda loves her son or at least as much as Sheila and Matt love me. When Sheila and Matt most love me, they won't say, "Dennis, we love you unconditionally, much more than you can ever imagine. But you know, Dennis, you really blew it. So, to hell with you, but remember how much we love you." And even though Sheila has a mighty big purse, she does not lug around an account book to mark down what I merit as punishment. And if Sheila and Matt don't do these unloving things, then God or our higher power will not do them either.

What Kind of God Is Our Higher Power?

The God of the 12 Steps and 12 Traditions is at least as loving as the God that I met through Hilda.[9] I hadn't known this. I had thought that the "higher power" in the Steps could be almost anything, even a vengeful, judgmental God. To a certain extent this is true, since 12 Step groups welcome everyone and all 12 Steps and 12 Traditions are merely suggestions. But Tradition Two suggests that the higher power is not just any God, but rather, a "loving" God, much like the one I met through Hilda.

> For our group purpose there is but one ultimate authority—a loving God as he may express himself in our group conscience.

Tradition Two says that if you want to experience what God is like, then experience our group conscience, or how we act when we live out the principles of our group. One way group conscience expresses itself is in A.A.'s government structure:

Where does A.A. get its direction? Who runs it? This too is a puzzler for every friend and newcomer. When told that our society has no president having authority to govern it, it has no treasurer who can compel the payment of any dues, no board of directors who can cast an erring member into outer darkness, that no member can give another a directive and enforce obedience, our friends gasp and exclaim, "This simply can't be. There must be an angle somewhere."[10]

In saying there is no board of directors who can cast an erring member into outer darkness, no treasurer who can compel the payment of dues, and no enforced obedience, Bill is describing not only how A.A.'s group conscience acts but also what their "loving God" is like.

First, there is "no board of directors who can cast an erring member into outer darkness." Tradition Three's commentary makes this even more clear by stating that at one time they were going to exclude everyone, from "beggars and tramps to plain crackpots and fallen women."[11] But instead A.A. ruled that anyone could be an A.A. member. "You are an A.A. member if you say so. You can declare yourself in and nobody can keep you out. No matter who you are, no matter how low you've gone, no matter how grave your emotional complications—even your crimes—we still can't deny you."[12] Twelve Step groups give everyone an unconditional welcome. Their "loving God," as expressed in group conscience, would do the same. The God of Tradition Two does not throw anyone into outer darkness.

Secondly, 12 Step groups have no treasurer who can compel payment of dues, which means there is no "you pay this in order to get that." There is "no enforced obedience." No one can punish or expel an offender.[13] Group conscience or the "loving God" of Tradition Two would never say "You do this or you get that, you act this way or you go to hell." Thus the "loving God" of 12 Step groups has no coercive merit system. All is free gift. Tradition Two hopes that as you experience group members welcoming you, especially when you were expecting judgment or even expulsion, you can experience how "the ultimate authority" or "the loving God" of 12 Step groups also treats you.

For years the 12 Steps alone did little to help me with my addiction to self-righteousness, because my higher power was not the loving God of Tradition Two. The Twelve Steps did set up a process for admitting I was powerless and helped me turn my life over to a higher power. But, my higher power at the time was as self-righteous as I was, and we become like the higher power we adore. I changed only when Hilda introduced me to a God similar to the loving God of the 12 Traditions. The way Hilda loved her son was an example of a person living out the characteristics of group conscience.

Vince, an A.A. member with forty-two years of sobriety, also gave me an image of how A.A.'s loving God acts through group conscience. When Vince first joined A.A., he saved no money because, he told me, "I traded my bar bill for travel and phone bills." Vince traveled all over his state attending A.A. meetings and looking for what he called the "big guns," alcoholics with many years of sobriety. Through the years he kept in contact with ten of these "big guns," often visiting or calling them especially when he felt confused about a decision. Now, all but one of the "big guns" have died.

But all ten remain part of Vince's life. Whenever Vince has a difficult decision to make, he starts through the names of the "big guns" and asks himself, "What would Eddie D. tell me to do? How about John R., or Jimmy S., or Terry D.? What would they tell me?" "You know," Vince said, "I only have to go through three or four of the names before I know exactly what to do. That's how I work Step 11 and come to know God's will for me and receive the power to carry it out." By listening to "group conscience" as it expresses itself through the "big guns," Vince experiences the essence of 12 Step spirituality: If you want to know what God's healing love is like, experience the love of those

who love you the most. Experience how Eddie D. would treat
Vince, or how Hilda would treat her son, or how Sheila and Matt
treat me. Then know that your higher power loves you at least as
much as those who love you the most.

IS CHRISTIANITY AS CHRISTIAN AS THE 12 STEPS?

Some in recovery may not be concerned about whether 12
Step spirituality has anything to do with Jesus and Christianity.
Generally such people know that the 12 Steps work, and for that,
they will be eternally grateful. This section is for those who feel
hesitant to become more deeply involved in 12 Step recovery
because, as they see it, "The 12 Steps are not Christian."

Although I believe that 12 Step groups are profoundly Christian, it is true that they welcome everyone, even atheists. In the
early days, however, A.A. members tended to judge such people
harshly.

> Ed was an atheist. His pet obsession was that A.A. could get
> along better without its "God nonsense." He browbeat every-
> body, and everybody expected that he'd soon get drunk—for
> at the time, you see, A.A. was on the pious side. There must
> be a heavy penalty, it was thought, for blasphemy. Distress-
> ingly enough, Ed proceeded to stay sober.
>
> At length the time came for Ed to speak at a meet-
> ing. . . . Cried Ed, "I can't stand this God stuff! It's a lot of
> malarkey for weak folks. This group doesn't need it, and I
> won't have it! To hell with it!"
>
> A great wave of outraged resentment engulfed the meet-
> ing, sweeping every member to a single resolve: "Out he
> goes!"[14]

To the dismay of some critics who wish that 12 Step groups
were more "Christian," A.A. decided that it must welcome even

atheists like Ed. But such critics miss how Bill and the group conscience of A.A. decided on their welcoming course of action toward Ed. In his commentary on Tradition Three, where Bill discusses difficult cases such as Ed's, Bill asks the core question for a Christian, "What would the Master do?"[15] Once they sensed what Jesus would do, Bill and A.A. also knew what they needed to do. They let Ed stay. This is an example of how not only individuals, but even organizations like A.A. become like the God they adore.

Some, especially those who like myself grew up with a judgmental God, may still struggle with the "loving God" of Tradition Two and the "Master" Jesus of Tradition Three who welcome everyone, even atheistic Ed. Just how Christian these Traditions really are is evident in the story of St. Paul (Acts 9:1–22). When Bill W. reflected on his own spiritual awakening, he identified with St. Paul's thunderbolt experience on the road to Damascus.[16] Bill understood how that experience brought Paul into a "new state of consciousness, and so opened the way to release from old problems." After my spiritual awakening with Hilda, I also thought of Paul on the road to Damascus.

One could imagine few harder-hearted people than Paul. As a rigid pharisee who saw the mistakes in everyone but himself, Paul was self-righteous like myself. Paul also behaved like a "control-aholic" and a "rage-aholic." Such people control their environment through violence against those who are different from themselves. Like Hilda's son or atheistic Ed, Paul wanted nothing to do with Jesus. He even actively persecuted Jesus (Acts 9:4) and showed no signs of repentance.

And what did Jesus, "the Master," do? Jesus broke through and loved and healed him. Paul, like Bill W. and myself, changed when through a spiritual awakening his image of God changed. Paul's pharisaical image of God changed to an image of God similar to the loving God of Tradition Two. Paul was no longer addicted to vindictive self-righteousness, violence and murder because he discovered that God wasn't either. And what had Paul done to bring about this healing? Nothing. God had demanded from Paul no prerequisites: no prior repentance, nothing. Paul's story reveals that the radical good news Jesus brought is not: God loves the repentant sinner. Rather the radical good news is: God loves and heals the unrepentant sinner. St. Paul, like most of us, could repent only after God loved and healed him through a spiritual awakening which changed Paul's understanding or image of God.[a] Hilda understood this and so do 12 Step groups. Twelve Step group lore has many stories of the creative ways that their members intervened on addicts who showed "no signs of wanting to reform."[17] Both the Christian God of the New Testament which Paul discovered and the loving God of Tradition Two say: Regardless of what you have done and even regardless of how unrepentant or closed to God you may be, we are going to do our best to love and heal you. That's what "the Master" always did and still does.

The Loving God of 12 Step Recovery vs. the Vengeful God of Scripture

Does the vengeful, punishing God of some scripture passages cancel out the loving God and "Master" of 12 Step recovery? For instance, Mt. 5:29 says that if your right eye is a temptation, it would be better to pluck it out than to have a vengeful God throw you into hell. Having read that passage, Hilda believed that God would certainly throw her son (who was involved in prostitution and many other sins with his right eye) into the

---

a) We are not saying that repentance is unimportant. Rather, our point is that it is not the case that we first repent and then God loves and forgives us. Rather, it is just the opposite. We can repent only because God has first loved us and healed us sufficiently (1 Jn. 4:10).

fires of hell. How can the vengeful God of such scriptures be understood in light of the Master and loving God of A.A.?

The vengeful punishment passages of the Bible confront us with the same question that confronted Bill W. in the subway: Is God a child abuser? Commenting on Step 11 Bill says that recovery involves our understanding of God moving away from that of a God who is a child abuser, "who doesn't know or care about beings," to a loving God. We believe recovery depends upon a radical choice: to accept a God who is a child lover and to reject a God who is a child abuser. When we read the vengeful punishment passages, we sometimes miss their meaning because we read them as if God were a child abuser and not a child lover. So how do we understand the Bible?

In his commentary on Tradition Two, Bill W. shares how at a group conscience meeting, members helped him discover how he was about to make a wrong choice as a result of reading the Bible literally.[b] Group conscience asks the question: What would those who love us the most do? So we might ask: How do those who love us most use vengeful punishment language? After asking this question I began to notice that those who love the most—grandparents, parents, lovers—often use the same words of vengeful punishment as child abusers, but with a very different meaning.

---

b) On the subway one evening, Bill thought he was receiving divine guidance. He heard a voice repeating a Bible passage, "The laborer is worthy of his hire." Bill believed that Bible passage literally. He thought it meant that he should leave his volunteer job with A.A. and, "since he was worthy of his hire," accept a job offer as a well-paid therapist at a New York hospital. The weekly A.A. meeting at Bill's home was that evening. Bill went to the meeting seeking approval for his decision through group conscience. The group told Bill that it would hurt A.A. if he and others became paid professionals. Bill concluded, "So spoke the group conscience. The group was right and I was wrong; the voice on the subway was not the voice of God. Here was the true voice, welling up out of my friends." Thus Bill admitted that he had been wrong to believe the Bible so literally, especially when it contradicted how those who loved him the most would act.[18]

For example, our cousin Ann and her husband George have raised four of the healthiest teenagers we know. So, whenever we're writing about family dynamics, we ask them, "How did you do it?" Recently we talked with Ann and George about punishment. We asked them, "When was the last time you punished your kids?" They both looked blank. So we said, "Can you remember any time in the past year when you punished your kids?" Still no answer. In desperation we asked, "When in the past five or ten years have you punished your kids?" They looked at each other and came up with the same thing. Ann said, "One time on a family trip, it got so loud in the back seat of the car that George said to the kids, 'If you don't be quiet, I'm going to tie you to the roof of the car!' And do you remember, George, how quiet it got?"

About that time their son, Joe, came home. We asked him the same questions and got the same blank looks. Finally, we asked, "Joe, can you remember any time at all in the past five or ten years when your parents punished you?" Joe's face lit up. "Dad, do you remember when we were in the car on a trip and we were making so much noise? You told us that if we weren't quiet, you'd tie us to the roof of the car!" Joe added, "And, boy, were we quiet. But we knew you weren't going to tie us to the roof of the car." And they all laughed.

To tie your children to the roof of a car is vengeful punishment. We use such vengeful punishment language all the time in families. But if, at the time people use it, they are really loving us, then they will never carry out the punishment.[c] The person to

---

c) We are not speaking here of "therapeutic punishment," in which we provide structure for a child who is physically or emotionally overwhelmed (e.g., sending a child who is overtired and fussy to its room for a nap), and/or in which we ask a child to take responsibililty for the consequences of its behavior (e.g., asking a child to pay for damage to another's property caused by the child's carelessness). Such therapeutic punishment is done lovingly and is intended to enable the child to give and receive more love. Vengeful punishment, on the other hand, is not done lovingly and does not enable anyone to give and receive more love.

whom the words are addressed knows that too. Everyone involved knows that the language is used only to emphasize the importance of doing something so that we can enjoy being together. Thus, in the car George was probably saying something like, "It's important that you be quiet so that we can enjoy the trip together." And in Mt. 5:29, instead of a command to pluck out your right eye, God may well be saying something like, "It's important that you not damage your right eye—the window to your heart—so that we can enjoy the inner beauty of creation together."[19]

On the other hand, what if Ann and George were child abusers who did tie their kids to the roof of the car? If I overheard them saying exactly the same thing to their kids, I would call the police. I would have the police put George and Ann (or God for that matter) in a mental institution before they could do more harm to their kids. But group conscience means that God is at least as loving as George and Ann. Like them, God is not a child abuser but a child lover and deserves to be listened to as such.

Rejecting a child-abusing God and moving toward an image of God as a child lover not only was crucial to Bill W.'s spiritual awakening and to the development of A.A., but was also the core of Jesus' mission. Jesus was always trying to change people's vindictive image of God. For instance, Jesus often wanted to heal on the sabbath, or touch a leper, or forgive someone. But the priests, scribes, and pharisees would quote him literally the vengeful punishment passages of their Bibles and forbid Jesus to do it. This infuriated Jesus.

In the story of the adulterous woman (Jn. 8:2–12), the scribes and pharisees are going to stone an adulterous woman to death. They tell Jesus, "Moses has ordered us in the law to condemn women like this to death by stoning" (Jn. 8:15). They are referring to Lv. 20:10 and Dt. 22:20, where God orders the vengeful punishment of stoning to death an adulterous woman. If Jesus, like the scribes and pharisees, had read such vengeful punishment passages literally, he would have had to join in stoning the adulterous woman. In inviting the scribes and pharisees to put down their stones, he is inviting them to stop reading the vengeful punishment passages of the Bible literally. Unfortunately, literal interpretation of the Bible did not end with the scribes and pharisees. In *Redemptive Intimacy*, Dick Westley quotes theologian Walter Imbiorski who describes one way it has been handed down to us:

> You see, part of the difficulty is that most of us are caught up emotionally in what I would call Anselmian Salvation Theology, which goes something like this. God created the world. Adam and Eve sinned. God got pretty damn sore, goes into a 10,000 year pout, slams the gates of heaven and throws the scoundrels out. So he's up there pouting and about 5,000 years go by and the Son comes up and gives him the elbow and says: "Hey Dad, now is the time to forgive those people down there." God says, "No. I don't like them, they offended my divine majesty, they stay out. Let's make another galaxy instead!" Five thousand more years go by and the Son comes up and says: "Aw come on, Dad, let's forgive them! Look, I tell you what I'm going to do. If you will love them again, I'll go down there and become one of them, then you'll have to love them because I'll be one of them." God looks at the Son and says: "Don't bank on it. That doesn't turn me on too much at all." So the Son replies, "All right, God-Father, I'll tell you what I'm going to do. I'll raise the ante. I'll make you an offer you can't refuse! I'll not only go down there and become one of them, I'll suffer for them, real blood—you know how that turns you on, Dad! How about it?" And God says: "Now you're talking. But it's got to be real torture and real blood—no God-tricks you understand. You've got to really suffer. And if you'll do that then I'll forgive them. But if they stray off the straight and narrow just that much— ZAP—I'm going to send them to hell so fast their heads will swim." And that is what we have been calling the "good news" of the Gospel. [20]

Prosecuting Attorney or Defense Attorney

The theology of Anselm (1033–1109) leaves out the "good news" because it ignores other traditional and more compassionate understandings of the New Testament accounts.[21] For instance, "parakletos" or the "Spirit of Jesus that judges us" could best be translated as "our defense attorney who justifies us" (Jn. 14:15, Jn. 15:26).[22] Spanish conveys this well, since in many biblical translations and church prayers it describes the Spirit of Jesus which judges as "nuestro abogado" or as "our defense attorney."

Jesus judges Paul, for example, as a defense attorney would. Jesus does tell Paul all that he did wrong including how he persecuted Christians. But rather than condemn Paul, Jesus understands the "justness" or reasonableness of Paul's life. Thus Jesus can heal Paul because he sees through to Paul's inner goodness. Jesus is Paul's defense attorney rather than a prosecuting attorney. Jesus is also the adulterous woman's defense attorney and refuses to let anyone else condemn or harm her. Two events that reveal Jesus' stance as defense attorney are his request at his death: "Father, forgive them; they don't know what they're doing" (Lk. 23:34), and his subsequent descent into hell (1 Pt. 3:19). In both events, Jesus' judgment of mercy places him in solidarity with condemned sinners.[d]

---

d) 1 Peter 3:19 is translated in the Jerusalem Bible as "descent into hell" and in other translations as "preaching to the spirits in prison." The common understanding of Jesus' descent into hell is that Jesus goes to hell to preach the good news only to the just souls awaiting redemption. However, theologian Hans Urs von Balthasar asserts that Jesus' descent into hell, commemorated each Holy Saturday, also signifies Jesus' utter solidarity with sinners. "At the same time, as the one who "descends into hell," Jesus is the expression of the radical unwillingness of God to abandon sinners, even where, by definition, God cannot be, insofar as hell means the utter and obstinate rejection of God."[23]

And exactly in that way he disturbs the absolute loneliness striven for by the sinner: the sinner, who wants to be "damned" apart from

A.A. evolved from understanding God as a vengeful prosecuting attorney to understanding God as a defense attorney. We have already referred to A.A.'s early struggle over whom to admit as an A.A. member.

> We resolved to admit nobody to A.A. but the hypothetical class of people we termed "pure alcoholics." Except for their guzzling, and the unfortunate results thereof, they could have no other complications. So beggars, tramps, asylum inmates, prisoners, queers, plain crackpots, and fallen women were definitely out. Yes sir, we'd cater only to pure and respectable alcohohlics![25]

Why did A.A. change its mind and welcome more than just the "pure and respectable alcoholics"? Bill's commentary on Tradition Three explains that to allow only pure and respectable alcoholics would be to vengefully punish all others by "pronouncing their death sentence . . . condemning them to endless misery." They concluded, "Who dared to be judge, jury, and executioner of his own sick brother?"[26] Ultimately A.A. abandoned all membership regulations and committed itself to welcome every alcoholic. Thus, A.A. members commit themselves to being not vengeful judges but rather defense attorneys on behalf of their own sick brother or sister.

This commitment to be like a non-judgmental defense attorney, welcoming all, is meant to be an expression of how a loving God behaves. This is evident from the final sentence of Tradition Three: "So the hand of Providence early gave us a sign that any

---

God, finds God again in his loneliness, but God in the absolute weakness of love who unfathomably in the period of nontime enters into solidarity with those damning themselves. The words of the Psalm, "If I make my bed in the netherworld, thou art there" (Ps. 139:8), thereby take on a totally new meaning.[24]

In our words, Jesus is the expression of God's desire to be our defense attorney.

alcoholic is a member of our society when he says so." A.A's God is a provident defense attorney speaking through A.A.'s group conscience, which is always on the side of the members.

Who Is the God That I Understand?

Many of us grew up in churches where God was not a defense attorney but rather a God of "fear and medieval superstition," much like the one Bill W. rejected. I grew up with fear and medieval superstition about afterlife. As I re-examine what I was taught, the conclusions I draw might be different from yours. But that doesn't matter. What matters is that we each come to terms with God as we understand God.

When I set aside medieval superstition, I discover that my Roman Catholic tradition and many Christian traditions hold two beliefs about afterlife. These beliefs are not the only Christian way to look at afterlife, but they are one doctrinally orthodox way. The first belief is that heaven exists and people are there. We all have loved ones—grandparents, parents, aunts and uncles—who we believe are in heaven. Secondly, hell exists as a possibility, but we don't know if anyone is there. If any people are in hell, it is not because God sent them there but because they chose it. C.S. Lewis used the image of hell as a room with the door closed from the inside, our side. But neither God, nor in my case the Roman Catholic Church, nor the Bible has ever said that anyone has chosen hell.[27] We know only that we are not to judge. We are to pray that all of us open our hearts to God.

What hope do we have that all people will open their hearts to God? What happens when we die? The God of the Old and New Testaments is an expert at opening hearts. For instance, we read how God, in Jesus, did thousands of miracles in just three years' time. Many of them were with hard-hearted people, like Paul, who wanted nothing to do with Jesus. When we die, we will have not just three years but a whole eternity of God's loving and healing initiatives. Even if we were to die as hard-hearted as Paul, God would spend eternity trying to love and heal us. We know this because God's essence is love and love heals. God has no other choice but to spend eternity loving and healing us (1 Cor 13).ᵉ

Some people say, "But we don't have a whole eternity. We make a free definitive decision at death,ᶠ when we choose either heaven or hell forever." Since none of us have died, none of us can know this with certainty. But let's just imagine that what they say is true. This would mean that at the moment of death we would have to experience a whole eternity of God's healing initiatives, because we cannot freely and definitively turn down what we have not experienced. Regardless of what happens at the

---

e) The optimism we express here is consistent with the consensus of current Roman Catholic theology. Karl Rahner and "virtually every other contemporary Catholic theologian" argue for an "unshakable hope" that in the end all men and women will be healed and will enjoy eternal life.[28]

f) Free will has often been defined as the ability to say "Yes" or "No" to God. However, Karl Rahner and other theologians suggest what seems to us a more profound understanding of free will, as the capacity to choose in a God-like way. Thus a truly free person can, paradoxically, like God, only choose the good. Saying "No" to God is not a sign of free will but rather of how a person still needs healing in order to become free. Once healed and truly free, that person, like Jesus, can only say "Yes" to God. This view has an understanding of the finality of persons similar to Meister Eckhart who wrote, "The seed of God is in us. Now the seed of a pear tree grows into a pear tree; and a hazel seed grows into a hazel tree; a seed of God grows into God." Thus,

. . . human freedom is simply and most radically the capacity for God, not the capacity for *either* God or something else. Human freedom is created for one end alone: God. Only God finally "defines" the human person. Therefore, it would seem that human freedom can attain real finality only when it reaches the definitiveness for which it is specifically created.[29]

Many observers of human development in the field of psychotherapy, such as Carl Rogers, agree that as hurts are healed, people become truly free and will always use their freedom to choose the good.[30]

moment of death, our hope is like that of an alcoholic attending his or her first meeting. Such an alcoholic's hope is not in the life she or he has lived but rather in the higher power or God of love and healing. That same image of a God who loves and heals is our hope in facing eternity. This, at least, is God as I understand God. What would your understanding be?

We Become Like the God We Adore

Why is it so crucial to come to terms with our understanding of God, and even change our image of God as I did? It is not so we'll know what afterlife is like. Rather, it is because we become like the God we adore. Studies show this is true in many aspects of our lives. In marriage, for example, the more a couple experiences God as a lover, the more likely they are to enjoy a wholesome, loving marriage. This wholesomeness extends to all aspects of marriage, including sexual fulfillment. Studies also show that the more we experience God as a lover, the more likely we are to consider social justice as "extremely important."[31]

As the churches have grown in realizing God's love for all, many of them have issued pastoral letters on peace, such as that written by the U.S. Roman Catholic bishops. Such pastorals say that we can never use nuclear weapons against our enemies. If my vengeful God can send enemies to a hell inferno, then I can send a nuclear inferno on my enemies. But as soon as God can't do it, I can't either.[g]

---

g) If we really believe there are people in hell, we can be tempted to populate it with those whom we find threatening, thus giving up on them. Hans-Jürgen Verweyen writes,

> Whoever reckons with the possibility of even only *one* person's being lost besides himself is hardly able to love unreservedly. . . .
> Just the slightest nagging thought of a final hell for others tempts us, in moments in which human togetherness becomes especially difficult, to leave the other to himself.[32]

Not just world peace but every social justice issue comes down to our image of God. For instance, our Catholic bishops just issued an economic pastoral which says that wealth or goods cannot be divided on the basis of what we merit through our work. Rather they must be divided on the basis of what we need. This may be difficult to accept if we have a vengeful, punishing God who calculates on the basis of our work exactly what we merit as eternal reward or punishment. In this case, our eco nomic system will probably also be based on merit. One can easily say to those who have less, "To hell with you, we earned it." But when God becomes a lover generously giving free gifts to those working only an hour (Mt. 20:1–16), and even to unrepentant sinners solely because they need it, then our economic system can also be based less on merit and more on need. Whatever our addiction as a society, whether it be to violence as opposed to peace, or to hoarding money as opposed to sharing, we usually mimic the addictions of the God we adore.

The most urgent reason to change our image of God comes from addiction itself. Whether our addiction be work, money, smoking or drinking, we begin every addiction for the same reason that Bill W. took his first drink: to deaden the pain of not belonging. To the extent that we have a God who can send us to hell, who can vengefully decide who doesn't get love and who doesn't belong, then we will probably become fearful and addicted people. At least I know that the more I feared God sending me to hell the more addicted I became.

Treatment centers recognize that the recovery rate is much lower for addicts with a punishing image of God. Dr. Robert Stuckey, whose recovery units have treated over 20,000 addicts, says that "God as we understand God" can be "tricky," because such a God "can be a punishing or a forgiving God." A personal, forgiving God is so crucial in the recovery process that Stuckey claims he has "never known a real hard-core heroin addict . . . to make it who didn't have a strong personal faith in God, using the term 'God,' not 'higher power.' " He concludes that addicts "with a very harsh view of God have a harder time than people with no religious training at all."[33]

When I speak of how our recovery depends so much on knowing God as merciful and loving, the most frequent question I am asked is this: "If God is so merciful and loving, then why be good?" I understand that question since I did many good things because I feared a vengeful, punishing God. For instance, I read Mt. 25 about the goats and sheep. I interpreted this passage literally and thought that since the goats go to hell and the sheep go to heaven, I wanted to make sure I was a sheep. So, out of fear and as a good sheep, I did many good things such as visiting the sick and feeding the hungry. Yet, when my image of God changed, I did even more good things and did them with more love. We do the most loving actions for those we love the most, not for those we fear the most. I do more for Sheila and Matt than for anyone else.

We can scare people into changing their behavior through fear of hell or fear of losing love. But such fearful behavior is not going to be loving behavior, because perfect love casts out fear. Fear may have to be used occasionally on an emergency basis. For instance, a family might tell their alcoholic father that unless he changes they are going to leave. Such fear of abandonment and of not belonging might get the alcoholic to stop drinking. But unless the alcoholic's fear of abandonment is replaced with a deep sense of love and belonging, he or she will replace drinking with other addictions. Through fear we can temporarily change a person's behavior, but only love and belonging can ultimately change the person.

Sheila, who grew up in the Jewish tradition and thus never had "the fear of hell" put into her, tells me that it never would have occurred to the Jews in her synagogue to scare people into being good. She says, "In our Jewish community, we knew that people were naturally good. If they did something that wasn't so good, it was only because they were hurt and scared. We knew that what these scared people needed wasn't more fear, but rather, more love and care from all of us."[34] Unloving behavior is not ok. But what heals it permanently is love, not fear. As Bill W. said, "Punishment never heals. Only love can heal."[35]

Our Image of God Keeps Evolving

The easiest way for me to keep growing in my image of God is to ask, "What has already helped most to change my image of God?" Whatever the answer, I do more of it. Sometimes I might find, as the native Americans do, that being with nature helps. Other times I might find that exploring the wonders of science or a new way of praying helps most. Often what helps me most is asking those that I love to share with me how God has transformed their lives. For instance, Sheila introduced me to the feminine side of God, especially God as Mother and God as Spouse. This has opened me more to the feminine, intuitive side of my personality and to my unconscious. Now, God the Mother speaks to me through my dreams. Whether it be with Sheila or with friends like Hilda, as I grow to love these people and appreciate how God transforms their lives, I "catch" and experience their God. The same thing happened to Bill W. when his friend Ebby shared his spiritual awakening with Bill.

These days, as I plant for the first time my own flower garden, I am aware of several people who taught me that the very earth is God's body. Recognizing how the earth is God's body has made me more sensitive to my connection to the earth and to ecological issues. One of the most difficult things Sheila and I did this year was to take a $3,000 reduction in our income, because to have earned that money we would have had to damage the ecology of our neighborhood. Just as 12 Step groups recognize a loving God as expressed through the "group conscience" of their members, I am recognizing a loving God as expressed through the "group conscience" of all creation. New images of God heal us to the extent that they put us in touch with a more loving God, since we can usually become only as loving or as recovered as the God we adore.

A SIMPLE WAY TO CHANGE OUR IMAGE OF GOD

Perhaps the easiest way to change our image of God is to try something that takes only a half minute.

1. Get in touch with the love of your higher power in your heart.
2. Put a smile on your face that matches that love.
3. Smile at a friend and allow that friend to smile back at you.

Taking in the smile of a friend is such a simple thing. Yet, it can be one of the most healing things in life if when we do it we know that God loves us, just for a start, at least as much as that friend. Because we become like the God we adore, the good news of 12 Step recovery is that of a loving God whose self-expression can be recognized in the group conscience or the smile of a friend. Adoring this kind of higher power, Bill W. says, will return to us a sense of belonging where "all will be well with us here and hereafter."

CHAPTER TEN

Step 12

12. Having had a spiritual awakening as the result of these steps, we tried to carry this message to others, and to practice these principles in all our affairs.

REFLECTION

Having entered this process of restoration through deepening my sense of belonging to my real self, God, others and the universe as members of my family, I shared this with others.

THE LOOP OF GIVING AND RECEIVING LOVE

While studying spirituality in Boston, as mentioned before, I (Matt) lived with Philip, a retired Jesuit who had twenty-five years of experience with A.A. Confined at home because of illness, Philip spent his days phoning fellow A.A. members. About ten times each week, Philip would tell me that he had just called another person who was going out the door to drink again. Finally I asked Philip how he knew whom to call. What radar did he have that could spot the shaky hands on the doorknobs? He laughed and replied, "That's easy. I just watch for those who aren't helping others to get sober and I call them. They are no longer getting life by reaching out and will soon be drinking again. That's the Twelfth Step." According to the psychologist

Erik Erikson, the same is true for all those in the stage of genera-
tivity (ages 35–65). Growth comes primarily by reaching out to
generate new life in another. When this doesn't happen in a
balanced way, a mid-life crisis often occurs.[1]

The Twelfth Step May Be Dangerous for Codependents

Bill W. wrote that this step of helping others kept him sober:

> In the first six months of my sobriety, I worked hard with
> many alcoholics. Not a one responded. Yet this work kept me
> sober. It wasn't a question of those alcoholics giving me
> anything. My stability came out of trying to give, not out of
> demanding that I receive.[2]

The Twelfth Step was Bill's favorite and he, unlike A.A.'s other
co-founder, Dr. Bob, spent a lifetime traveling to help other
alcoholics. Yet because helping others was Bill's gift, he also hurt
himself by overusing this gift. After Bill stopped drinking, he fell
into an eleven-year depression. It developed as his life became
overloaded with caring for A.A. Writing on Step 12, Bill's ideal is
expressed in his advice on how to approach a drinking alcoholic:
"Suggest how important it is that he place the welfare of other
people ahead of his own."[3] No one had yet defined this ideal as
codependency. Finally Bill sought help from a psychiatrist who
recognized how Bill hurt himself through his need to help others.
Without using the name "codependency," his psychiatrist identified the lethal pattern in Bill, who writes:

> Her thesis is that my position in A.A. has become quite
> inconsistent with my needs as an individual. Highly satisfac-
> tory to live one's life for others, it cannot be anything but
> disastrous to live one's life for others as those others think it
> should be lived. . . . The extent to which the A.A. move-

ment and individuals in it determine my choices is really astonishing. Things which are primary to me (even for the good of A.A.) are unfulfilled. I'm constantly diverted to secondary or even useless activities by A.A.'s whose demands seem to them primary, but are not really so. So we have the person of Mr. Anonymous in conflict with Bill Wilson.[4]

Fortunately Bill took the advice of his psychiatrist. He stopped taking responsibility for so many others and instead cared for his own needs. When Bill turned the leadership of A.A. over to the Service Committee, he came out of his depression. The Twelfth Step brings life when lived in balance and not with a codependent's compulsive need to help others.

Since codependency fuels the addictive cycle and keeps us from getting help, the Twelfth Step of giving must be balanced by receiving. Our Reflection stresses the receiving through reconnecting that fills us with so much life that it overflows to others:

Having entered this process of restoration through deepening my sense of belonging to my real self, God, others, and the universe as members of my family, I shared this with others.

Life must be received and given in a continuous loop, just as we have to breathe in and out.

Should I Reach Out More or Less?

My healing occurs as I both give and receive with others. For example, when we give weekend retreats, I spend several hours at night hearing confessions. As I hear others confessing the same sins I have, I feel God's love and forgiveness not just for them but for myself too, and I get new life. But after two hours of confessions, I start to wish the line would end so I can get to bed. Then I treat the next person as a problem to be solved with quick advice rather than as a person to walk with in his or her pain. That person senses my fatigue and begins with a guilty "I'm sorry it's so late. Do you have time to hear me too?" Neither they nor I receive much life, and we are both eager to finish. When that is happening I am overextended and need to stop and receive life rather than keep giving more.

When it is time to reach out and give, it always brings life both to me and to the other person. It is time to stop when it no longer generates life in both of us. Giving must have a loop of receiving or it is unhealthy codependency. Melody Beattie says we are codependent caretakers when we are "consistently giving more than we receive in a particular situation."[5] If I am giving because I *should*, rather than because I enjoy it, usually I am breaking the loop and treating the other as an inferior victim whom I condescend to help. Several questions help me recognize when this is occurring:[6]

1. Am I giving help that I don't want to give (and I feel like a victim who may then turn angry persecutor)? For example, "I'd rather be in bed than hearing confessions so hurry up and finish."

2. Am I teaching others to help themselves (rather than perpetuating victims)? For example, am I encouraging them to give and receive forgiveness with others in their lives?

3. Do I look down on others who aren't giving as much as I (because I feel like a victim giving more than my share)? For example, am I angry that other priests quit hearing confessions at 10 P.M. as we had scheduled, and left me with a long line?

4. Am I giving help that others don't need (and keeping them from finding their own solutions)? For example, people may

substitute confession for getting in touch with themselves in therapy.

5. Am I getting life from this or feel I am giving more than I am receiving?

If I don't ask these questions on a night when I am hearing confessions, as described above, I lose an opportunity to give the most valuable gift I have: my real self—in this case, my honest "No." If I tell people in a confession line, "No, I can't listen to you because I'm exhausted," my "No" is a gift because it communicates permission for others to say "No" and models for them a vulnerable ability to express needs and set limits.[a]

Because I have learned to express my own needs and limits, and have been able to balance giving and receiving life, I have traveled nine months a year for the past fifteen years in over forty countries without ever suffering burnout. We have a rule that when we travel in a foreign country, we always reserve half the time just to receive.

This may sound like permission to do only what we enjoy and to avoid whatever is unpleasant. Growth sometimes involves choosing to do what is not enjoyable, e.g., a parent who gets up to change a diaper at 3 A.M. However, such inconveniences promote growth only when they are part of a larger commitment that we do enjoy. For example, pediatrician Dr. T. Berry Brazelton says that a mother and child will bond to the degree the

---

a) Despite Bill W.'s overemphasis on giving mentioned earlier, he demonstrated this kind of honesty about one's own needs during his first "Twelfth Step Call." When Bill W. and Dr. Bob went to visit Bill D. (who became the third member of A.A.), they made it clear that they needed to talk to another alcoholic in order to stay sober themselves. While Bill D. had resented others who had previously come to him *for his good*, he appreciated Bill W. and Dr. Bob's honest admission of their own self-interest and he was therefore willing to listen to them.[7]

mother enjoys being a mother.[8] He wants mothers to stay home with infants. He also concedes that a mother who works and wants to be with her baby is probably a better mother than the one at home who wants to work but feels trapped into baby-sitting. This mother at home, although physically present, is not really emotionally present for bonding. Love that forms a loop, bonds. Brazelton sees so many mothers not bonding with their children that he warns, "We are raising a generation of terrorists!"

Reaching Out To Change Structures

Giving and receiving life often calls me not only to reach out to persons but also to change oppressive structures. As I do so, I grow in freedom from addictive behavior. On November 16, 1989, the El Salvador army (with the foreknowledge of the local U.S. Major General) brutally murdered six of my brother Jesuits, their cook and her daughter. The army murdered the Jesuits for attempting to promote dialogue between the government and the guerrillas. At the University of Central America, the Jesuits had spoken out against abuses on both sides. Fearing the Jesuits' search for truth, their murderers scooped out the victims' brains, as a sign to everyone not to pursue such thinking.

As we heard the news, I and my Jesuit community fell into a depression. When my American government, despite prior knowledge of the murders, allowed it to happen and then blamed it on guerrillas (although the university area was under army control and not guerrilla control the night of the murders),[9] my addictions returned as they did when I lived in the oppressive Bolivian environment. I became enmeshed in compulsive nega-tivity and snacking. I worked twenty hours a day, stuck in a perfectionism that demanded constant rewriting and always more preparation for the next retreat. Even attending 12 Step meetings didn't heal my despair. They helped me feel it more, name it and accept what I couldn't change. Yet I still longed to change whatever could be changed. Then I took a day to write letters to ten U.S. government officials. I demanded that military aid to El Salvador be tied to an investigation of the murders and to upholding human rights. Having done what I could to change structures, my despair and depression left and so did my addictive compulsions.

I notice something similar in women with whom I work. They are often freed from swallowing their pain, through overeating and other addictions, as they do what they can to change the abusive, power-seeking, patriarchal U.S. system which makes us the world's leading arms dealer rather than investing in childcare.

Throughout this book we have said that denied painful feelings create an inner division, an empty place between us and our real self. Our addictions come and fill that empty place. Joanna Macy suggests that one of the feelings most denied in our culture is despair for the world.[10] She believes that because we are connected to all life, we feel everything that happens on our planet. All of us care about environmental destruction, hunger, human rights abuses, etc., but we have no energy to act. Because we repress our despair over the suffering around us, we don't have access to its creative energy. When I first learned about the murder of the Jesuits and the women, I ran from my feelings and tried to escape through addictive behavior. Later, when I could be with my despair at such hideous injustice, and ask what could I change, my despair gave me the energy to write to government officials. I wonder if I was experiencing a moment of recovery from the denial of despair in our entire culture.

I carry this social despair as a burden that I often don't recognize until it is removed. For example, on August 19, 1991, a coup removed Russian President Gorbachev. That morning I felt as I had in the 1950's when I hid under school desks during air raid drills, after Khrushchev vowed to bury America. As Yeltsin leaped on a tank and rallied the people, I was glued to the television, praying for the bus barricade to stop the advancing army. What a celebration four days later when the coup failed and Gorbachev was reinstated! My body heaved a sigh of relief as if shedding a huge burden. The despair that lifted in those four days is the unconscious despair I had lived with during four decades of cold war. What despairing burden am I denying now and will only know when it is removed?

Growing up with the threat of nuclear holocaust was an experience of abuse for my entire generation. The roots of addiction lie in abuse, whether conscious or unconscious. The Twelfth Step heals these roots as we become aware of them and reach out not only to individuals but also to change the unjust social structures that abuse us.

Reaching Out Heals Our Hurts

Giving and receiving new life by reaching out also heals hurts. I believe more than ever in the power of the Twelfth Step, because it was reaching out that healed me after Dennis left our Jesuit house to marry Sheila. Although I knew Dennis had to follow his conscience, I sank into depression as I faced the loss of twenty-seven years of sharing the same Jesuit life, nearly all of those years living and working together. My superior gave me good advice: live where you will be most loved and do what will give you life. So I stayed in Omaha among loving friends.

I was afraid to continue giving retreats. It seemed too painful to speak of healing hurts. Also, Dennis and Sheila had taken six months off, and during that time I would have to give retreats alone. I knew that my talks would be only one-third as good as giving a retreat with Dennis and Sheila. Instead of trusting that reaching out heals, I dreamed of being a hermit and tried to cancel the retreats that I would have to give alone.

I most wanted to cancel a Spanish retreat in San Diego

because we were depending on Dennis' excellent Spanish and he would be absent. I have studied Spanish for only seven months, so I speak like a seven-month-old baby, and I hadn't used it at all for a year. So I called the retreat coordinator and said I was cancelling because I couldn't speak Spanish. Besides, they had other Spanish speakers. She replied that many were coming to hear me. So if I couldn't speak Spanish, she would get me a translator. I couldn't back out of that since my English is ok. I accepted, but I also asked to come three days early so I could live with a Spanish family. I hoped after three days to understand Spanish again even if I couldn't speak it.

I arrived in San Diego to stay with an elderly couple, Jesús and Maria Fernandez. I heard lots of Spanish because they could speak no English. I felt so loved by them that I spent three days speaking broken Spanish without fear of making mistakes. I thanked Jesús for his patience and told him I was looking forward to speaking English at the conference. In English I could say ten times more than in Spanish. He shocked me with his response:

> The leaders want you to speak Spanish, not English. The people will understand enough of your Spanish just as I do. We know you can speak ten times better in English, but we aren't interested in hearing ten times more. The important thing is not how much you give but how much we feel your love. If you speak in English we will miss your heart because it will be coming through another's heart.

Since that failed to convince me, Jesús continued,

> Let me tell you an old story my grandfather told me. A rich man and a poor man each had five sons. The rich man died and left each of his sons a whole ranch. So the poor man's sons jokingly asked their father what they would inherit, since there was scarcely enough bread for each day. The poor

man said to his sons, "Go down to the river and each bring
back two jarilla branches." [The jarilla is like a willow with
branches as thick as a finger.] When they returned, the poor
man said to his sons, "Now break one of your branches."
Each did that easily. "Now bring me the other branches." He
then took the five remaining branches and tied them into a
bundle. Then he handed the bundle to the oldest son. "Now
break it." Neither the elder son nor any of the sons could
break the bundle. The poor man then took the bundle, "This
is the inheritance I give you. In unity there is strength (la
unidad hace la fuerza)."

Then Jesús looked at me and added, "That's why we don't need
you to give big gifts in English. We need to become one with you
as you love us with your heart in Spanish."

The next day I spoke to the assembly in my broken Spanish:

I am here to tell you that you are to use your gifts to evangelize, pray for the sick, and help those in need. How many of
you feel ready to step out and do it? [Only a few raised their
hands.] That's normal. We always feel someone else can do
it better. Some of you are looking at me and thinking that
you can't evangelize or pray as well. [Heads nodded.] I am
looking at you and certain that each of you can speak, evangelize, and pray in Spanish ten times better than I can. By now
as you hear a mistake in every sentence, you know that too.
Yet I am the one giving this talk and risking using my little
gift. I wanted to give this talk in English rather than Spanish.
But Jesús said to me, "The important thing is not how well
you do in English but how much you love with your little gift
of Spanish."

Then I told them the story of the jarillas and how what counts is
not the size of the gift but each of us using our little gift with great
love. They understood immediately and applauded. I felt so

much love that I continued speaking for another twenty minutes from my heart. Receiving their love healed me and called forth a talk I didn't know I could give.

After the talk I received un monton de abrazos (a mountain of hugs) and invitations to speak to other Spanish groups. Each hug said to my fearful bones that I could step out and give retreats without worrying whether they would be as good as before. The important thing was to risk using my inadequate gift and let the reaching out continue to heal me as it did that day. I didn't have to be a hermit.

So I believe in the Twelfth Step, not just because it helps others but because it has healed me. Without it I wouldn't have risked giving new talks on the 12 Steps and now, as a result, writing this book. The Twelfth Step is also why I am not waiting to write this until I am perfectly prepared. When I get tempted to wait until I have read twenty more books, I recall the Twelfth Step and try to break my bundle of five jarillas.

SEALED ORDERS

Our recovery depends not only on giving and receiving life in the Twelfth Step, but on giving and receiving life in our own special way. For example, Jack McGinnis has a wonderful gift for creating an atmosphere in which the little child within each person feels safe. For the past several years, Jack's full-time work has been giving 12 Step retreats. When we attended one of these retreats, what impressed us most was the atmosphere of safety Jack created. He also has a gift for music. Recently various song producers have expressed interest in professionally recording Jack's music and distributing it to radio stations. Jack told us how good he has felt about his life since he began using his two favorite gifts, and that he no longer feels the chronic shame he had felt previously.

Many people working in the field of recovery believe that the core feeling in addicts and in people from dysfunctional families is chronic, toxic, internalized shame. When shame is internalized, we disown our real self. Deep within we may think, "I am not being my real self. I am not doing with my life what I was sent here to do. I am not sharing my gifts with others."

Agnes Sanford, a pioneer in the field of healing, said that every person comes into this world with "sealed orders" from God. To us, this does not mean that God gives us orders in a militaristic way. Rather, it's as if, before we were born, each of us talked over with God the special purpose of our time on earth. Throughout our lives we discover more and more deeply our unique sealed orders, a way that only we were gifted to give and receive love. During Bill W.'s first meeting with Ed Dowling, the Jesuit priest (who would become Bill's spiritual mentor) helped Bill get in touch with his sealed orders. Ed

> . . . looked straight into Bill's eyes . . . he told him that the two of them in that little room were among the blessed of all time, for they were here, living now. Out of those who had gone before, and all those not yet born, they had been elected to stand up now and speak their piece. There was a force in Bill that was all his own, that had never been on this earth before . . . [11]

People who were wounded in childhood and therefore got caught in addictive patterns have had to use all their energy to survive. There is very little left over, it seems, to carry out those sealed orders. That is how it seemed to me. I (Sheila) was so deprived emotionally that I could not grow up on schedule. Even as a small child, I thought despairingly, "I will never get caught up to where I'm supposed to be. I'm so far behind." I knew I was here for some special reason, and I was afraid I would fail both God and myself.

Bill W. describes a similar fear among alcoholics: "The spectacle of years of waste threw us into panic. There simply wouldn't be time, we thought, to rebuild our shattered fortunes."[12] After seventeen years of drinking, Bill thought he had wasted his life. However, Bill's long struggle with alcoholism became the core of his special gift to this world.

Our sealed orders are built into us so deeply that they can lead us back to the direction of our life no matter how many mistakes we've made or how far behind we think we are. All our life, we're trying to carry them out. Something leads us from within, and uses the very mistakes we've made to help us.

As a child I experienced severe deprivation and abuse. But even in the midst of it, my sealed orders were leading me to life. I handled my pain by wandering off alone in the woods, looking at leaves or blades of grass. In school, I stared out the window at the sky. I felt drawn into the special goodness of leaves, grass, sky, etc. I was taking in the beauty of those things to survive emotionally, since there wasn't much beauty in my home. The adults around me did not understand what I was doing. They only knew I was extremely withdrawn. Finally, when I was fifteen, the school guidance counselor became so concerned that she arranged to have me sent to live with my grandparents. I never lived with my parents again. I had to leave their home to survive, and the way that I did it was by looking at beauty and appreciating it. I used the sealed orders of my life to help me.

The sealed orders of my life are to be present to the unique goodness of each thing exactly as it is, and by my loving presence to help it become more itself. Even when I felt the most despair that I would never get caught up, that special gift within me was leading me out. It was showing me the way home, it was crying out to the guidance counselor for help, it was trying to phone home like E. T.—it saved my life.

Each of us has a special way of giving life, our own sealed orders. They were built into the cells of our bodies and can lead us out even when we think there is no hope for us. The way we know our sealed orders is by the joy we feel when we begin to fulfill them, and by the way everything in our lives falls into place. In his series of interviews with Joseph Campbell, Bill Moyers asks,

> Do you ever have this sense when you are following your bliss, as I have at moments, of being helped by hidden hands?

Joseph Campbell answers,

> All the time. It is miraculous. I even have a superstition that has grown on me as the result of invisible hands coming all the time, that if you do follow your bliss you put yourself on a kind of track that has been there all the while waiting for you, and the life that you ought to be living is the one you are living. When you can see that, you begin to meet people who are in the field of your bliss, and they open doors to you. I say, follow your bliss and don't be afraid, and doors will open where you didn't know they were going to be.[13]

We all know the way home. We all know the phone number, like E.T. We all have built into us a special way that we're called to give and receive life, and that will lead us back to where we belong.

WHAT IS YOUR NAME?

Understanding our sealed orders often evolves. For instance, this year during a car trip Sheila and I (Dennis) listened to a tape by Robert Johnson. He said that the word "monk" expresses the purpose of his life. Once he discovered this, he could stop putting unfair expectations upon himself to be everything. He could focus on what he was meant to be. After hearing that, Sheila and I decided to turn off the tape and see if we could discover our sealed orders in a word or "name."

To discover my word, I began with the question: "When lately have I felt as if I really belonged?" I remembered my last two Minnesota fishing trips. I love to go out on the transparent, still Minnesota waters, put a worm on the dropline, and watch the sunfish nibble on my hook. Another memory of belonging had the same feel as fishing in still Minnesota waters. That was my two-year discernment process at the Jesuit Retreat Center in Guelph which ended with the decision to marry Sheila. During that process, I plummeted the depths of my unconscious through a combination of dream work, gestalt, primitive drawing and a thirty-day Ignatian retreat. Each day, I felt keen anticipation as I dropped my line into the still waters of the unconscious to catch another surprise revelation. That is why I drew on our wedding invitation what Sheila and I consider the symbol of our marriage: two people together in a boat, fishing with droplines for sunfish and other treasures. For us, fishing in still waters symbolizes a quiet transparency that we have always shared with each other. From these and other moments of belonging, I eventually came up with two words that seemed to capture this part of my essence: "still waters." That's how I felt inside myself and that's what the space felt like that I made for another in those moments of belonging.

These two words felt right, so I excitedly shared them with Sheila. She told me she had expected me to come up with the words "dancing heart." My excitement over my "still waters" discovery waned as I recalled that several years ago Sheila and I had done a similar exercise. As Sheila correctly remembered, I had come up with the words "dancing heart." "Dancing heart" expressed how I felt one hot day in Mexico when I led a liturgy for garbage pickers who lived in the garbage dump. They were celebrating the anniversary of their garbage pickers' co-op. During that liturgy we all joyfully danced in the dust of the dump.

"Dancing heart" captured for me a zest I have for life, and my ability to find goodness in even the darkest and most forsaken places, including garbage dumps. I wished Sheila hadn't reminded me about "dancing heart." Both images felt right to me. I like to have things clear, and it seemed to me that Sheila had just muddled them up.

The next day we continued our trip and listened again to Robert Johnson. He said that "Dennis," or "Dionysius" in Greek, means "ecstasy." As he described the various facets of "ecstasy," I realized that "ecstasy" captures my sealed orders. "Dancing heart" and "still waters" are the two ways "ecstasy" most manifests itself in my life. What really amazed me is that when we finally arrived that night, our hosts had just finished Robert Johnson's book, *Ecstasy*.[14] I didn't know that he had written such a book. When I read it, I knew that he was writing about me.

My understanding of my sealed orders keeps evolving. Although "ecstasy" seems now to describe the purpose of my life, I wouldn't be surprised if soon something else will describe my life even more accurately. Discovering our sealed orders is like a journey closer and closer to the core of who we were meant to be. Perhaps the meditation that follows will help you begin your journey of discovering your sealed orders.

NAMING OUR SEALED ORDERS

1. Place your hand on your heart and ask your higher power to bring to your heart a moment in your life when you felt as if you belonged. Maybe it was your marriage, the birth of your child, or a moment of reconciliation with a friend. Share with your higher power in a sentence or two what was special about that moment. What did people say or do that helped you feel as if you belonged?

2. Breathe in that feeling of belonging. Fill your whole body and feel what it is like in every cell.
3. What word or name does your higher power have for your special gift, or sealed orders? If it seems appropriate, let your higher power anoint you to deepen that gift.
4. Take a moment or two and imagine yourself reaching out to others with the gift of your sealed orders. Breathe in the feeling of wholeness and belonging that it gives you.

Appendix A: Using the Imagination for Healing and Recovery

In this book we have spoken of many ways we can open ourselves to the power of the 12 Steps, e.g., through loving relationships, grieving, finding the genius beneath the addiction, etc. We want to add one more tool for recovery: the imagination. Noting that alcoholics had used imagination to "create reality out of bottles," Bill W. said their problem was not imagination itself, but their "almost total inability to point imagination toward the right objectives. There's nothing the matter with constructive imagination; all sound achievement rests upon it."[1] According to addiction specialist, Mark Mitchell, "Unless an individual can *see* himself or herself sober, he or she can't stay sober."[2]

Many who work in the field of healing now recognize the power of the imagination. For example, Dr. Bernard Siegel can predict which children will be exceptional cancer survivors based on how they express imagination in art work.[3] The child who can imagine and draw his or her immune system as easily defeating the cancer cells has a much better chance than the child imagining a pitched battle.

Mark Mitchell describes the role of the imagination in recovery:

Within the last 20 years more research has been done in the functions of the mind/brain. The research has found that the brain often functions like a movie camera. We accumulate a high proportion of information through visual experience and then create outside behavioral realities to match our internal visual picture.

This explains a lot. Sometimes we will hear from people new in recovery, "I just can't see myself sober." These people really can't. They have lost or been unable to create internal visual pictures of themselves sober; as a result, they don't stay sober. Unless an individual can *see* himself or herself sober, he or she can't stay sober.

What can be done? Several things. First, continued involvement in the spiritual and social aspects of a Twelve-Step program. Second, it's good to take some time during the day to relax and create a fantasy of sobriety. This can be achieved by simply closing the eyes, focusing on the breathing, and seeing oneself going through day to day life sober. It is important to visualize colors, what is being said, what is being heard, along with a feeling of relaxation and contentment at being sober. Third, if in the course of this exercise pictures of drunkenness emerge, it is important to deal with these pictures and their features. Frequently imagining these drunken pictures shrinking while sober pictures get larger and more vivid can have a positive effect.

Fourth, it is important to recognize that when pictures of drunkenness or getting loaded emerge, they represent a force that needs to be respected. It was often during drunken episodes that alcoholics found themselves complete or alive. This desire for completion or aliveness needs to be met in non-alcoholic ways.[4]

Note that it is necessary to respect the fantasies of acting out the addiction, e.g. drunkenness. Through these fantasies, the imagination offers ways to uncover the roots of the problem and heal them.

Patrick Carnes, the leading authority for the treatment of sexual addiction, relies on the imagination to prevent relapse:

Treatment centers and therapists have long worked with sex addicts on developing strategies to prevent relapse when slips occur. Often these are called dress rehearsals or fire drills. Some have criticized this approach as giving permission to slip by planning for it. Yet such strategies truly acknowledge the addict's powerlessness and the "cunning and baffling" nature of the illness. Planning for the inevitable moment of weakness is an important discipline for recovering people if they are to minimize risk and prevent further damage.

One standard strategy used by therapists involves three phases. First, the addict is asked to describe the perfect acting-out fantasy. This gives the addict and the therapist a chance to figure out the scenarios that govern the addiction. Every addict's acting out is based on some script, usually programmed by the family or an abuse experience or some powerful childhood sexual experience. When the addict details what would make it perfect, the seeds of compulsivity and destruction become clear. These then can be resolved therapeutically.

In the second phase, the addict imagines and records what the consequences would be if the fantasy were to become a reality. All possibilities must be specified. By doing this, the addict starts to contaminate or spoil the fantasy. Addicts do not link their fantasies to the consequences. Making the link reduces both the power of the fantasy and the addict's vulnerability to relapse.

In the third phase, the therapist has the addict think about what he or she will do if a slip does occur. What if the fantasy and its consequences become reality, wreaking havoc in the addict's life? What plan of action exists? Once the addict starts to slip, he or she will be tempted to say, "Well, I've gone this far, why not go all the way?" A slip can then become a binge or a return to the addictive life. An exit strategy is a way out of this downward spiral. It allows the recovering person to go into "automatic pilot" and focus on damage control. Usually, this exit strategy takes the form of a contract with a therapist or sponsor. The contract specifies what the addict agrees to do if a slip occurs.[5]

Perhaps this sounds very complicated: imagining the perfect acting-out fantasy, resolving the therapeutic issues in it, recording all the consequences of the fantasy, and forming imaginative solutions for every possible slip. All this helps, but we don't have to be in therapy or a treatment center to begin tapping the imagination's power. We can start in a small way by taking one compulsive behavior and imagining the next step in recovery.

For example, I (Matt) have shared my process of recovery from my addiction to anger (Chapters Four and Six). The next step for me is dealing with my self-righteousness that never wants to apologize. Lately, this too has begun to change as I use the power of the imagination. In the past, I would answer another's confrontation by defending myself and then getting locked into a debate.

Lately I have tried to imagine myself apologizing when I am wrong. This past week I pulled up thistles for Sheila. I tried to be careful not to step on any other plants because part of Sheila is hurt when any plant gets hurt. Later Sheila came in and told me I trampled some of her favorite plants. My instinctive reaction was to say that I tried to be careful and to blame the neighbor's dogs. Fortunately, I had been imagining how good it felt to apologize when I needed to do so. As I imagined myself apologizing, I felt integrity and strength that could correct mistakes. Without effort I found myself saying to Sheila that I was sorry I stepped on the plants because I knew how much they meant to her. That night Sheila told me she found me more open to correction and to apologizing than ever before. If that is true, I owe it all to the power of my imagination to develop new possibilities where previously I was compulsively stuck.

The reason I tried imagination when I was stuck in anger is that I find it helpful in ministry with others. I often ask a person what she feels God most wants to empower her to do. Then I tell her to breathe in God's power and imagine the new behavior while I pray silently for this to occur. For example, one woman could not clean her basement because she had been sexually abused in a basement. Although she had worked on this in therapy, she still got headaches after just a few minutes of trying to clean the basement. When I asked her how God wanted to empower her, she imagined herself sweeping the basement. She felt tall and filled with yellow light. She saw herself as able to create an environment rather than be controlled by one. When she returned a month later, she told me she had not only cleaned the basement but also painted it in the yellow of the light she imagined in the prayer. She could spend hours there feeling peace instead of headaches. When I have done this with others stuck in sexual compulsions, food addictions, etc., they have shared with me how imagination helped them, too, to take the next step in recovery.

What we have said about the imagination parallels Bill W.'s description of a spiritual awakening as a new state of consciousness where one believes, feels and does what previously was impossible. While reading Bill's description, perhaps imagine it happening— and it will be the beginning of a spiritual awakening.

> When a man or a woman has a spiritual awakening, the most important meaning of it is that he has now become able to do, feel, and believe that which he could not do before on his unaided strength and resources alone. He has been granted a gift which amounts to a new state of consciousness and being. . . . He has laid hold of a source of strength which, in

one way or another, he had hitherto denied himself. He finds himself in possession of a degree of honesty, tolerance, unselfishness, peace of mind, and love of which he had thought himself quite incapable. What he has received is a free gift, and yet usually, at least in some small part, he has made himself ready to receive it.[6]

Appendix B: Course Guide

Below is a suggested format for using this book (and accompanying tapes, if you wish) as a course lasting ten weeks or more. Using this format with a group (defined as two or more people up to any number), you can:

a) come to the group meeting already having read the week's chapter in this book and/or listened to the corresponding audio tape, or

b) during the meeting listen to as much of the week's audio tape as you wish, or watch the videotape (see Group Experience, Part B, below). Audio tapes are up to ninety minutes long, and can easily be broken up into two or three parts that can be used at two or three meetings. Parts of the tapes correspond to the sections in this book. Times are marked on the audio tape labels. Videotapes are thirty or forty minutes long.

This format takes one to two hours for each of the sessions. Feel free to vary the format to meet the needs of your group. You may also wish to vary the frequency of meetings, e.g., meet every two weeks or perhaps have several sessions over one weekend. Each member of your group will need a copy of this book, and, if you use the audio or videotapes, the group will need at least one set.

I.   GROUP EXPERIENCE
    A.   Common Opening Prayer (5 minutes)
        E.g., you may wish to take a moment of silence and then pray the Serenity Prayer:

218

Lord, grant me the serenity to accept the things I cannot change, the courage to change the things I can, and the wisdom to know the difference.

B. Audio or Videotape (approximately 30–40 minutes, optional)

If you are using tapes and are choosing to include them in the group meeting, listen to (or show) a tape from the series *Belonging*.

C. Silent Reflection (5 minutes)

Quiet time to get in touch with what part of the written and/or taped material for this week moved your heart most deeply.

D. Guided Journaling (10 minutes; see example on pp. 143–145)

1. Write down what is in your heart. Write as if you were writing a love letter to your best friend—your higher power—sharing what you feel most deeply. Don't worry about having the "right" words, but only try to share your heart. If drawing is more helpful for you than writing, draw a picture or symbol to express what you feel.

2. Now get in touch with your higher power's response to you, as he/she is already speaking to you within. You might do this by asking what are the most loving words that you could possibly hear, or by imagining that what you have just shared is a note or drawing for you from the person you love most and you want to respond to that person in the most loving possible way.

3. Write (or draw) your higher power's response. Perhaps it will be just one word or one sentence. You can be sure that anything you write (or draw) which

helps you to know that you are loved is really from your higher power.

4. One or two people might want to share what they have written or drawn with the whole group. During the Companion Sharing time which follows, companions may wish to share with each other what they have written.

E. Companion Sharing (5 minutes minimum for each person to share his or her reaction to this week's written and/or taped material and to the Home Experiences during the past week. By the second session, each person should choose one or two companions for Companion Sharing and Companion Prayer. If possible, companions should remain together throughout the course.)

1. Share with your companion as much as you wish of what is in your heart after seeing/hearing this week's tape and/or reading this week's chapter in the book.

2. Share with your companion your experience with the Home Experiences during the past week. You may also wish to share from your journal.

3. What are you most grateful for now and how do you need your higher power's help?

F. Companion Prayer (5–10 minutes of prayer for each person) Pray in your own way, either aloud or silently, for what your companion most needs. If it feels right to both of you, as you pray you may wish to lay your hands on your companion or take his or her hand. Then let your companion pray for you.

G. Group Sharing (15 minutes or more)
Share with the whole group your response to this week's

tape and to the Home Experiences of the previous week.

H. Closing Snack and Celebration (optional)
An open-ended time to enjoy one another and to continue sharing.

II. HOME EXPERIENCES

A. Daily Healing Prayer (a few minutes or as long as you wish) Each day share some quiet time with your higher power. The following prayers are *suggestions*. Perhaps you will find yourself drawn to pray what is in your heart using varied breathing, a symbol, a repeated word, a melody, a gesture, a drawing, or a piece of clay which you can mold. Perhaps your prayer will be as simple as looking at a beautiful flower and taking in God's love for you. There are over two hundred suggested ways to pray in our book *Prayer Course for Healing Life's Hurts* (see Appendix C).

1. Do the prayer process at the end of this week's tape and/or book chapter. Or, return to any previous prayer process in the course or in the rest of your life that you have found helpful.

2. Breath Prayer. Sit erect, feet flat on the floor, hands on your lap, palms up. Become aware of the sensations in your body (e.g., tension in your shoulders, a knot in your stomach, etc.). Breathe deeply, feeling the air as it passes into your nose and down to your lungs. As you inhale, breathe in whatever you most need from your higher power. As you exhale, breathe out whatever you most want to entrust to your higher power. As you breathe, you may want to silently repeat a word, phrase or scripture that is meaningful for you.

3. Embrace Prayer. See your higher power or a nurturing friend standing before you, or seated in a rocking chair. See such persons open their arms and invite you to them. Go to them, letting them hold you and perhaps rock you in the chair. Feel their arms around you and let yourself be loved as if you were a small child.

4. Reparenting Prayer. Recall a recent experience when you behaved in an unfree way. Recall the moment immediately before you did it. What did you need in that moment? Now think of a person who has what you need. In your imagination, be with this person and breathe in what you need from him or her. Is there a way this person or someone else can continue to give you what you need?

B. Daily Journal (5 minutes)

1. Share with your higher power when during this prayer or during the day your heart was deeply moved—perhaps a moment of being grateful for or of longing for healing in being able to do one of the 12 Steps or in being present to another who struggles with this Step.

2. Write (or draw) in your journal your higher power's response. If you can't get in touch with your higher power's response, express what most moves you as you share yourself with your higher power, or what are the most loving words you want to hear.

C. Reflection Question

Using your own words, how would you write a Reflection on the Step(s) of this week's lesson?

D. Scriptures
   If scripture is healing for you, following are some suggestions:

Step 1:	Lk. 15:14–16	The prodigal son, unlike the elder brother, admits being powerless.
	2 Cor. 12:9	Power is made perfect in weakness.
Step 2:	Lk. 15:17	The prodigal comes to his senses.
	Rom. 8:11	The same power that raised Jesus from the dead is at work within us.
Step 3:	Lk. 15:18	The prodigal decides to return home.
	Rom. 8:38	Nothing can separate us from God's love.
Step 4:	Lk. 15:18–19	The prodigal faces what he has done.
	Lk. 1:39–56	Mary acknowledges her connectedness.
Step 5:	Lk. 15:20–21	The prodigal admits the nature of his life to his father.
	Ps. 139:14	I am wonderful.
Step 6:	Lk. 15:22–24	As soon as the prodigal confesses, his father restores his losses.

	Lk. 24:13–35	Healing and restoration come as grief is shared with Jesus at Emmaus.
Step 7:	Lk. 15:25–32	Because of hurts, the elder son refuses to embrace the restoration process.
	Eph. 3:14–21	Prayer for our real self to be restored.
Step 8:	Lk. 15:19	The prodigal wants to make amends.
	Mt. 19:13–15	Jesus welcomes and heals the children that adults scold.
Step 9:	Lk. 15:22–24	The prodigal comes as a wounded child and accepts the father's gifts.
	Lk. 19:1–10	Zacchaeus makes amends as his wounded inner child is understood, respected, and offered a chance to have a party.
Step 10:	Eph. 4:25–28	Anger is good; deal with its underlying hurts daily before the sun goes down.
	Lk. 17:11–19	The leper's gratitude for the present event is a sign of true healing.
Step 11:	Lk. 15:8–10 & 11–32	Two images of God throwing a party, feminine and masculine.

	Jn. 8:2–12	Jesus challenges a vengeful image of God.
Step 12:	Jn. 21	Peter is healed and called back to his sealed orders.
	Lk. 10:25–37	The outcast Good Samaritan reaches out to a wounded outcast.

Appendix C: Resources for Further Growth

Books

Healing the Eight Stages of Life, by Matthew Linn, Sheila Fabricant & Dennis Linn (Mahwah, NJ: Paulist Press, 1988). Based on Erik Erikson's developmental system, this book helps to heal hurts and develop gifts at each stage of life, from conception through old age, and is especially helpful for inner child work. Includes healing ways our image of God has been formed and deformed at each stage.

Healing of Memories, by Dennis & Matthew Linn (Mahwah, NJ: Paulist Press, 1974). A simple guide to inviting Jesus into our painful memories to help us forgive ourselves and others.

Healing Life's Hurts, by Dennis & Matthew Linn (Mahwah, NJ: Paulist Press, 1978). A more thorough book to help the reader move through hurts using the five stages of forgiveness.

Healing the Greatest Hurt, by Dennis & Matthew Linn and Sheila Fabricant (Mahwah, NJ: Paulist Press, 1985). Healing the deepest hurt most people experience, the loss of a loved one, by learning to give and receive love with the deceased through the Communion of Saints.

These and other books by the authors are available from Paulist Press, 997 Macarthur Blvd., Mahwah, NJ 07430, (201)825-7300.

Courses (for use alone, with a companion, or with a group)

Belonging: Healing & 12 Step Recovery, by Dennis, Sheila & Matthew Linn (Kansas City, MO: Credence Cassettes, 1992). Audio tapes to accompany this book. (See below for information on videotapes.)

Healing the Eight Stages of Life, by Matthew Linn, Sheila Fabricant & Dennis Linn (Mahwah, NJ: Paulist Press, 1985). Tapes and a course guide which can be used with book (see above) as a course in healing the life cycle. Available on videotape and in two audio versions, condensed and expanded.

Prayer Course for Healing Life's Hurts, by Dennis & Matthew Linn and Sheila Fabricant (Mahwah, NJ: Paulist Press, 1983). Ways to pray for personal healing that integrate physical, emotional, spiritual and social dimensions. Book includes course guide, and tapes are available in video and audio versions.

Praying with Another for Healing, by Dennis & Matthew Linn and Sheila Fabricant (Mahwah, NJ: Paulist Press, 1984). Guide to praying with another to heal hurts such as sexual abuse, depression, loss of a loved one, etc. Book includes course guide, and tapes are available in video and audio versions. *Healing the Greatest Hurt* (see above) may be used as supplementary reading for the last five of these sessions, which focus on healing of grief.

Dying to Live: Healing through Jesus' Seven Last Words, by Bill & Jean Carr and Dennis & Matthew Linn (Mahwah, NJ: Paulist

Press, 1983). How the seven last words of Jesus empower us to fully live the rest of our life. Tapes (available in video or audio versions) may be used with the book *Healing the Dying*, by Mary Jane, Dennis & Matthew Linn (Mahwah, NJ: Paulist Press, 1979).

Audio tapes for all of these courses (except *Belonging*) are available from Paulist Press, 997 Macarthur Blvd., Mahwah, NJ 07430, (201)825-7300. *Belonging* audio tapes are available from Credence Cassettes, 115 E. Armour Blvd., Kansas City, MO 64111, (800)444-8910.

Videotapes for all of these courses (except *Belonging*) may be purchased from Paulist Press. For information on *Belonging* videotapes, contact Christian Video Library, 3914-A Michigan Ave., St. Louis, MO 63118, (314)865-0729.

Videotapes on a Donation Basis

To borrow any of the above videotapes, contact Christian Video Library at the above address.

Spanish Books & Tapes

Several of the above books (including this one) and tapes are available in Spanish. For information, contact Christian Video Library.

RETREATS & CONFERENCES

For retreats and conferences by the authors on the material in this book and other topics, contact Dennis, Sheila & Matthew Linn, c/o Re-Member Ministries, 3914-A Michigan Ave., St. Louis, MO 63118, (314)865-0729.

Notes

PREFACE

1. For a discussion of the roots of A.A.'s emphasis upon experience rather than absolutes, see Ernest Kurtz, *Not-God: A History of Alcoholics Anonymous* (Center City, MN: Hazelden, 1991), 26, 35, 45, 103–105, 117, 191.

2. *The Grapevine* (March, 1958), quoted in *As Bill Sees It*, (New York: Alcoholics Anonymous World Services, 1967), 45.

3. Kurtz, *op. cit.*, 99. See Kurtz, pp. 24, 50–52, 61, 99, and 152–53 for the importance of religious tolerance in A.A., and 175–230 for a discussion of its religious roots. One branch of the recovery movement, Rational Recovery, does reject faith in God. Cf., "Clean and Sober—and Agnostic," *Newsweek* (July 8, 1991), 62–63. Generally, however, 12 Step groups are extremely supportive of religious faith and also extremely unwilling to prescribe the content of that faith for any one person. Bill W. wrote, "A.A.'s tread innumerable paths in their quest for faith. . . . You can if you wish make A.A. itself your 'higher power'. . . . You will find many members who have crossed the threshold just this way. All of them will tell you that, once across, their faith broadened and deepened. Relieved of the alcohol obsession, their lives unaccountably transformed, they came to believe in a Higher Power, and most of them began to talk of God." *Twelve Steps and Twelve Traditions* (New York: Alcoholics Anonymous World Services, 1953), 27–28. Perhaps the best introduction to A.A.'s atti-

tude toward religion remains the classic chapter "We Agnostics," in *Alcoholics Anonymous* (New York: Alcoholics Anonymous World Services, 1976), 44–57. In this chapter Bill W. stresses the importance of forming "your own conception of God" and deciding what spiritual terms "mean to you." We believe this attitude is profoundly Christian and a protection against spiritual abuse. See Chapter 9 of this book.

4. *As Bill Sees It, op. cit.*, 34.

CHAPTER ONE: BILL W. AND THE SEARCH FOR BELONGING

1. Robert Thomsen, *Bill W.* (New York: Harper & Row, 1975), 8–10.

2. Thomsen, *op. cit.*, 28.

3. Kurtz, *op. cit.*, 309.

4. William Wilson, *Alcoholics Anonymous Comes of Age* (New York: Alcoholics Anonymous World Services, 1979), 53–54.

5. *'Pass It On'* (New York: Alcoholics Anonymous World Services, 1984), 56.

6. *Ibid.*, 121.

7. Thanks to Jack McGinnis for pointing out to us this similarity.

8. Kurtz, *op. cit.*, 125. Last part of quote originally appeared in *Twelve Steps and Twelve Traditions, op. cit.*, 105.

9. *'Pass It On', op. cit.*, 136. See also Kurtz, *op. cit.*, 26–27 and ff., and Thomsen, *op. cit.*, 234–236.

10. Wilson, *Alcoholics Anonymous Comes of Age, op. cit.*, vii, 59.

11. Nan Robertson, *Getting Better: Inside Alcoholics Anonymous* (New York: Fawcett Crest, 1988), 75.

12. The 1980 Rand Study was a four-year longitudinal study

of 920 alcoholics. Cited in Lewis Andrews, *To Thine Own Self Be True* (New York: Doubleday, 1987), 154. Other informal statistics indicate that 29% of A.A. members remain sober for more than five years, "a record considered enviable in the field." Reported in "Clean and Sober—And Agnostic," *Newsweek, op. cit.*, 63.

13. Barbara Yoder, *The Recovery Resource Book* (New York: Simon & Schuster, 1990), 225. Some credit the women's consciousness-raising movement with broadening the scope of self-help groups beyond alcoholism. Cf., "Unite and Conquer," *Newsweek* (February 5, 1990), 54.

14. Yoder, *op. cit.*, 10.

15. Pia Mellody with Andrea Wells Miller and Keith Miller, *Facing Codependence* (San Francisco: Harper & Row, 1989), xx.

16. Patrick Carnes, *Don't Call It Love* (New York: Bantam, 1991), 106 & 108. See also pp. 100, 263, 266.

17. Gershen Kaufman, *Shame: The Power of Caring* (Rochester, VT: Schenkman, 1985), 163–64.

18. *Twelve Steps and Twelve Traditions, op. cit.*, 80.

19. See Jack McGinnis & Barbara Shlemon, *The Truth Will Set You Free* videotape series and workbook, available from: Be-Loved Ministry, P.O. Box 1587, Torrance, CA 90505.

20. A conscious, felt sense of this connectedness may be absent in persons who have been emotionally deprived and who have impaired object constancy (the ability, even under stress, to maintain a stable image of one's primary caretaker as composed of both good and bad qualities). A felt sense of connectedness to the source of our life (whatever we call it) is normally restored when such emotional wounds are healed. Cf. Conrad Baars, *Born Only Once* (Chicago: Franciscan Herald Press, 1975), 53, and the work of John Gartner cited in "God and the Inner Image of Mother," *Common Boundary* (July/August, 1989), 30. According to Bill Wilson, "deep down in every man, woman and child is the fundamental idea of God." *Alcoholics Anonymous, op. cit.*, 55.

21. Dr. Graham Farrant attributes this to "cellular memory." Cf. "Cellular Consciousness and Conception: An Interview with Dr. Graham Farrant," *Journal of Christian Healing*, Vol. 11, No. 3 (Fall, 1989), 17–18. David Chamberlain's theory is that "brains, like televisions, are *tuning* devices" and that "storage of memory is outside the body-brain." Cf., David B. Chamberlain, "The Expanding Boundaries of Memory," *ReVision*, Vol. 12, No. 4 (Spring, 1990), 17 & 11. See also his book, *Babies Remember Birth* (New York: Ballantine, 1990) and Linda Mathison's account of children who shared pre- and perinatal memories with their parents, in "Birth Memories: Does Your Child Remember?" *Mothering* (Fall, 1981), 103–107.

22. Stanislav Grof, "Modern Consciousness Research and Human Survival," *ReVision* (Summer/Fall, 1985), 35–36.

23. Karl Pribram's theory of prenatal memory (which we think could be extended to include evolutionary memory carried in the sperm and the egg) is that memory depends on protein molecules in the single cell rather than on complex neural connections. Cited in Frank Lake, *Tight Corners in Pastoral Counseling* (London: Darton, Longman & Todd, 1981), 2 & 36. See also Graham Farrant, *op. cit.*, 17–23.

24. Robertson, *op. cit.*, 23, 27, 70.

25. The following passage suggests that Bill was aware of how such early hurts affected him in later life. Writing in 1958, he is still searching for the same things he lost when his girlfriend Bertha died, "romance, security and applause" (see page 7 of text): "Those adolescent urges that so many of us have for top approval, perfect security, and perfect romance—urges quite appropriate to age seventeen—prove to be an impossible way of life when we are at age forty-seven or fifty-seven. Since AA began, I've taken immense wallops in all these areas because of my failure to grow up, emotionally and spiritually." From "The Next Frontier: Emotional Sobriety," in *The Language of the Heart: Bill*

W.'s Grapevine Writings (New York: The A.A. Grapevine, 1988), 236.

26. In letters to friends written in 1953, Bill described himself in terms of what today we would call codependence. See Kurtz, *op. cit.*, 214.

27. *Alcoholics Anonymous, op. cit.*, 164.

28. Bill saw the temptation to believe one had the final answer as part of what he called "alcoholic grandiosity" and the tendency of addicts to think in absolutes. Sobriety for an individual and health for A.A. as a whole required acknowledging "limited con trol," which included the humble admission that no human being has the final answer, and a willingness to continually learn from new experience. Cf. Kurtz, *op. cit.*, 105–117.

29. For a discussion of the Roman Catholic understanding of giving and receiving love with the deceased through the communion of saints, see Matthew Linn, Dennis Linn & Sheila Fabricant, *Healing the Greatest Hurt* (Mahwah, NJ: Paulist Press, 1985). Included are perspectives from non-Roman Catholic sources, e.g., "A Presbyterian View," by Dr. Douglas Schoeninger, pp. 192–196.

CHAPTER TWO: TWO OF OUR STORIES

1. Patrick Carnes, *Don't Call It Love, op. cit.*, 76.

2. G.B. Spanier & P.C. Glick, "Paths To Remarriage," *J. of Divorce*, 3:283–298 (1980).

3. Sam Keen, *Fire In The Belly* (New York: Bantam, 1991), 137.

4. A recent article on support groups discusses their special relevance for contemporary American life: " . . . most professionals, and, of course, support group members themselves, see the meetings as an amazingly effective antidote to aloneness—

something that, apart from being a problem in its own right, compounds every known condition brought on by late 20th-century living, from compulsive hand-washing to AIDS." "Unite and Conquer," *Newsweek* (February 5, 1990), 50.

5. Henri Nouwen, *Gracias!* (New York: Harper & Row, 1983).

6. Bill Wilson speaks of alcoholics as tempted to either of two extremes, "guilt and self-loathing" or "self-righteousness or grandiosity." *Twelve Steps and Twelve Traditions, op. cit.*, 45–46. Pia Mellody discusses these same two extremes as symptoms of codependency, in *Facing Codependence, op. cit.*, 78–79, 111–113.

7. Thomas Holmes and Richard Rahe, "The Social Readjustment Scale," *J. of Psychosomatic Research*, 11 (April, 1967), 213–18.

ARE YOU GETTING STUCK?

1. *As Bill Sees It, op. cit.*, 98.

CHAPTER THREE: HOW DO ADDICTIONS BEGIN?

1. Jane R. Hirschmann, "Raising Children Free of Food and Weight Problems," *Mothering* (Summer, 1989), 27–31.

2. For a beautiful example of how a child must set limits on adults who overcontrol its eating, or risk eating disorders in later life, see "The Child Sets Limits" in Alice Miller, *Banished Knowledge* (New York: Doubleday, 1990), 176–180.

3. *Alcoholics Anonymous, op. cit.*, 23.

4. Gerald May, *Addiction & Grace* (San Francisco: Harper & Row, 1988), 24 and 11.

5. Letter from Bill Wilson to Purnell Handy Benson, April 25, 1961. Cited in Kurtz, *op. cit.*, 381. See also p. 217. The

context of Bill's statement is that he saw alcoholism as a metaphor for the sickness of modern culture in its insatiable craving for money, prestige and power.

6. May, *op. cit.*, 38–39.

7. Substance addictions (e.g., to alcohol, drugs, food, etc.) are normally distinguished from process addictions (e.g., to gambling, sex, relationships, anger. etc.) in that typically only the former are seen as having a biochemical basis. However, current research on the relationship between emotions and brain chemistry questions this distinction. Gerald May describes how *every* habitual behavior causes "feedback, habituation and adaptation," changes in brain chemistry similar to those caused by a substance addiction. In fact, an addiction that involves major areas of one's life, such as a relationship or workaholism, can sometimes affect larger systems of brain cells than a substance addiction. Cf. May, *op. cit.*, 83–85.

Patrick Carnes discusses the role of endorphins (brain chemicals) in sexual addiction (normally considered a process addiction). Sex addicts are, in a sense, getting high on their own brain chemicals. Carnes also discusses how the trauma of abuse may affect brain chemistry: "Research shows profound alterations in the neuropathways of the brain of trauma victims. These changes involve brain chemicals that are fundamental to the neurochemistry of addictions . . . " Cf. Carnes, *Don't Call It Love, op. cit.*, 22, 25, 30–34, 69–72, 336–337.

From our point of view, the significance of this resarch is that the need for emotional healing that is obvious in process addictions cannot be dismissed as irrelevant in substance addictions simply because they have a physiological component, since *all* addictions have a physiological component. Physiological intervention, however (e.g., medication), will not solve the underlying emotional issues.

8. Cf. Earnie Larsen, *Stage II Recovery: Beyond Addiction* (San Francisco: Harper & Row, 1985).

9. Ernest Kurtz, *op. cit.*, quoting Bill W., distinguishes the two stages as follows: "The first was that of the 'merely dry' former obsessive-compulsive drinker who 'put the cork in the bottle' yet continued to 'think alcoholically,' i.e., to entertain grandiose plans and expectations, to nurse feelings of resentment, etc. In 'true sobriety' or 'serenity,' one embraced a 'new way of life'; i.e., abandoned grandiosity, resentments, and other claims to be 'special,' and became aware that one's only true dependence was on the 'Higher Power'—that the *whole* program of the Twelve Steps of Alcoholics Anonymous was to be utilized in *all* aspects of daily life". (p. 123) These ideas are developed by Bill in *Living Sober* (New York: Alcoholics Anonymous World Services, 1975). The process of moving from one stage of recovery to the next is beautifully described in Patrick Carnes' longitudinal study of recovering sex addicts, *Don't Call It Love, op. cit.*

10. *Alcoholics Anonymous, op. cit.*, 22–23. Bill's doctor, William Silkworth, agreed. Although he was one of the early proponents of the theory of a physical allergy as causing alcoholism, in his later writings he deemphasized this theory and spoke more about "recovery as possible only on a moral basis." In his essay "The Doctor's Opinion" in *Alcoholics Anonymous* (p. xxvii), he wrote of the need for psychic transformation if the alcoholic was to have any hope of recovery. Cited in Kurtz, *op. cit.*, 22.

11. 1986 survey cited in Barbara Yoder, *The Recovery Resource Book, op. cit.*, 158.

12. *Ibid.*, 275. See also Carnes, *Don't Call It Love, op. cit.*, 106, 108, 129, 336.

13. Yoder, *op. cit.*, 178.

14. See, for example, Terry Kellogg, *Broken Toys Broken Dreams* (Amherst, MA: BRAT, 1990), 61–62, 64, 73, 78–79, 85, and Pia Mellody, *op. cit.*

15. Kaufman, *op. cit.*, 163 and ff.

16. John Bradshaw, *Healing the Shame That Binds You* (Deerfield Beach, FL: Health Communications, 1988), 97.

17. Carnes, *Don't Call It Love, op. cit.*, 94.

18. Patrick Carnes, *Contrary to Love* (Minneapolis: Comp-Care, 1989), 128.

19. Carnes used the Olson Circumplex Instrument, which posited sixteen family types by focusing on two aspects of family health: 1) adaptability, ranging from chaotic to rigid leadership, and 2) cohesion, ranging from enmeshed families (extreme emotional closeness) to disengaged families (extreme emotional distance). Carnes, *Contrary to Love, op. cit.*, 103–131. See also Carnes, *Don't Call It Love, op. cit.*, 106, 122–123.

20. Carnes, *Contrary to Love, op. cit.*, 127.

12 STEPS AND 12 REFLECTIONS

1. Letters from Bill Wilson to Charles W., June 3, 1952, and to Howard E., February 6, 1961. Cited in Kurtz, *op. cit.*, 356. See also Kurtz, 105–117, 266–267 and 277, and endnote 28 of Chapter 1 of this book.

2. *Alcoholics Anonymous, op. cit.*, 164.

CHAPTER FOUR: STEPS 1, 2, AND 3

1. The concept of aversion addictions can include "phobias, prejudices, bigotries, resistances, or allergies." May, *op. cit.*, 36. Some addictions experts refer to aversion addictions as "anorectic" conditions, and would identify my fear of women as "sexual anorexia." See, for example, Anne Wilson Schaef, *Escape from Intimacy* (San Francisco: Harper & Row, 1989), 13–18.

2. Tad Guzie, *Jesus and the Eucharist* (Mahwah, NJ: Paulist, 1974), 156.

3. Robert Thomsen, *op. cit.*, 329.

4. *Alcoholics Anonymous, op. cit.*, 55.

5. We see "embracing our powerless behavior" as the love

and welcome that St. Ignatius describes as the primary freeing grace of the first week of the *Spiritual Exercises* (the retreat process of four stages or "weeks" developed by Ignatius and commonly used today). For Ignatius, retreatants experience the grace of the first week when they both recognize their brokenness and experience themselves as loved unconditionally with that brokenness. Ignatius' "Rules for the Discernment of Spirits" say that once this happens, the retreatant will have a natural movement toward the greatest good and away from former compulsions. The pull of former compulsions will now be experienced as jarring rather than natural. This makes sense from our viewpoint of shame fueling compulsions, because shame is healed when we know that we are loved at our worst.

6. We believe this is another way of expressing an awareness that is foundational to recovery: trying to control an addiction never works. "The hallmark of addiction is a loss of control, marked by attempts to control. Addicts are very controlling people and very controlled people. They control feelings, the people around them, and try to control their addiction with repetitive, futile efforts. In some ways, the healthiest part of their lives can be their addiction, because it's the one part of their life where they're out of control. . . . The paradox of addiction is what we think we need the most of is really what we need the least of. We think we need to get in control and we try to control the addiction. *The most common recovery for addiction is addiction* because when we try to control the addiction that we have, another addiction tends to break out." Kellogg, *op. cit.*, 76–77. See also Kurtz, *op. cit.*, 105–111, 120, 122. Efforts to control addictions result not only in another addiction, but also in the "Shame Cycle" of "acting in" and "acting out," in which the addict alternates between being compulsively in control and compulsively out of control. Cf. Carnes, *Don't Call It Love*, *op. cit.*, 104–106, 235–239.

For a beautiful discussion of making friends with an addiction, see May, *op. cit.*, 155–161.

7. *'Pass It On'*, *op. cit.*, 384. Jung's 1961 letter included Psalm 42:1 as a footnote, "As the hart panteth after the water brooks, so panteth my soul after thee, O God." Years earlier, in 1940, during Bill's first conversation with Ed Dowling, S.J., the Jesuit priest (who became Bill's spiritual mentor) quoted from St. Matthew's gospel: "Blessed are they who hunger and thirst." Dowling suggested to Bill that his thirst for alcohol was really a thirst for the divine. This idea was a great comfort to Bill, and became one of Dowling's greatest gifts to Bill and through Bill to A.A. Cf., Mel B., *New Wine: The Spiritual Roots of the Twelve Step Miracle* (Center City, MN: Hazelden, 1991), 13, 148.

8. *'Pass It On'*, *op. cit.*, 385. See also *As Bill Sees It*, *op. cit.*, 323.

9. *Twelve Steps and Twelve Traditions* (New York: Alcoholics Anonymous World Services, 1953), 139.

10. Bill Moyers and Robert Bly, "A Gathering of Men" (New York: Mystic Fire Video, 1990).

11. Kathleen Hurley & Theodore Dobson, *What's My Type* (San Francisco: Harper & Row, 1992), p. 194 of manuscript (Chapter 6).

12. This is an example of what is commonly called "inner child work" or "dialoguing with the inner child." Relating to one's inner child as if to a distinct person can be carried to extremes, and some people working in the recovery field are concerned about the danger of dissociation. It seems well to remember that the inner child is not an entity separate from the self, but rather the child aspect of the whole person, to be integrated with the adult aspect of the person.

13. Focusing was originally developed by Eugene Gendlin at the University of Chicago. See his book *Focusing* (New York: Bantam, 1978). We learned focusing from Peter Campbell and Edwin McMahon, who have integrated it with Christian spirituality. We disagree with Campbell & McMahon in that we believe reparenting (from another person or from one's higher power) is

an important form of healing not allowed for in their presentation of focusing. Otherwise, we recommend their work. For an excellent brief introduction, see Peter Campbell, "Focusing: Doorway to the Body-Life of Spirit," *Creation Spirituality* (May/June, 1991), 24, 26, 27, 50, 52. For a listing of books and retreats, write Institute for Bio-Spiritual Research, 6305 Greeley Hill Rd., Coulterville, CA 95311.

14. See Kellogg, *op. cit.*, 64.

15. From the newsletter of the Institute for Bio-Spiritual Research, *Kairos*, 5:1 (Winter, 1990), 1–2.

16. Charlotte Kasl, *Models of Recovery* (Charlotte Kasl, Box 7073, Minneapolis, MN 55407), 22–23.

INTRODUCTION TO STEPS 4, 5, 6, AND 7

1. 1957 letter in *As Bill Sees It*, (New York: Alcoholics Anonymous World Services, 1967), 140.

CHAPTER FIVE: STEPS 4, 5, 6 AND 7
RESTORING OUR LOSSES THROUGH BELONGING

1. Joe McQ. & Charlie P., *Big Book Seminar* audio cassette series.

2. *Twelve Steps and Twelve Traditions*, *op. cit.*, 57. See also Kurtz, *op. cit.*, 124–128; "Emotional Sobriety," in *The Grapevine* (January, 1958); *Twelve Steps and Twelve Traditions*, *op. cit.*, 42–54, 115–116, 123; Robert J. Ackerman, *Children of Alcoholics: A Guidebook for Educators Therapists, and Parents* (Holmes Beach, FL: Learning Publications, 1983), 76.

3. Kurtz, *op. cit.*, 97; *Twelve Steps and Twelve Traditions*, *op. cit.*, 48.

4. Baars, *op. cit.*, 5–11.

5. *Ibid.*, 95; Conrad W. Baars, M.D., "The Alcoholic Priest," *The Priest*, Vol. 27, No. 6 (1971), 49–55.

6. See, for example, Kellogg, *op. cit.*, 73, 79, 85, and 103 on lack of relationship with one's real self as the root of addiction; Carnes, *Don't Call It Love*, *op. cit.*, 94–106; Kaufman, *op. cit.*, 163–165.

7. Baars, *op. cit.*, 114; Miller, *op. cit.*, 140–141.

8. Moyers & Bly, "A Gathering of Men," *op. cit.*

9. John Bowlby, *Attachment and Loss, Volume I: Attachment* (New York. Penguin, 1978), xiii.

10. Barry & Janae Weinhold, *Breaking Free of the Codependency Trap* (Walpole, NH: Stillpoint, 1989), 125.

11. Cf., Baars, *Born Only Once*, *op. cit.*, 19–23, 43, 53, 76–80, 98, 116–117. For what seems to us a balanced discussion of self-affirmation vs. affirmation from others, see Kaufman, *op. cit.*, 119–159.

12. Baars, *Born Only Once*, *op. cit.*, 26–27.

13. *Ibid.*, 32–42.

14. For a discussion of the difference between healthy and toxic shame, see John Bradshaw, *Healing the Shame That Binds You*, *op. cit.*, 3–23.

15. Pia Mellody describes the transfer of shame as follows: ". . . when a caregiver abuses a child, the caregiver is out of touch with his or her own healthy shame. . . . If the caregiver could feel healthy shame, he or she would stop abusing the child. As a result of being abused by a shame-filled parent out of touch with his or her shame, the child somehow develops a core of shame induced by the parent during the abuse. . . . The child's own shame gives him or her a sense of fallibility, but adding the parent's shame to the child's shame gives the child an overwhelming sense of worthlessness, 'badness,' and inadequacy." In *Facing Codependence*, *op. cit.*, 96–99. On "need-shame binds," see Gershen Kaufman, *Shame*, *op. cit.*, 44ff. On shame about one's

own dependency needs as a core symptom of codependency, see Kellogg, *op. cit.*, 1–2, 61–62, 64, 78, 147, 197.

16. Weinhold, *op. cit.*, 125.

17. Conrad W. Baars, M.D. & Anna A. Terruwe, M.D., *Healing the Unaffirmed: Recognizing Deprivation Neurosis* (New York: Alba House, 1976), 4.

18. Julian Meltzoff & Melvin Kornreich, *Research in Psychotherapy* (New York: Atherton Press, 1970), 203, 331, 334.

19. Thomsen, *op. cit.*, p. 227; Ernest Kurtz, *Not-God, op. cit.*, 15, 22.

20. Pia Mellody, *Facing Codependence, op. cit.*, 204. Pia (like most 12 Step veterans) goes on to recommend that the sponsor be a person of the same sex, to avoid the danger of romantic or sexual involvement. We understand and support this concern, yet we are also aware of the need for both motherly and fatherly reparenting. Reparenting a person of the opposite sex does require a high level of personal maturity and psychosexual integration. On the importance of affirming relationships for recovery, see also Carnes, *op. cit.*, 262–278.

21. We are suggesting a temporary, "healthy dependency" for purposes of reparenting. We trust this process, with two cautions. First, in our experience, the most common reason why such relationships sometimes get stuck in unhealthy dependency is that needy people may seek reparenting from those who do not really have the capacity to give it—and, conversely, helpers who are themselves unaffirmed may unconsciously seek a sense of self-worth and importance by encouraging needy people to remain dependent upon them. In a healthy reparenting relationship, the helper (like any healthy parent) 1) encourages the development of healthy autonomy in the other as his or her emotional needs are accepted and cared for; 2) gives emotionally, rather than taking in the guise of giving (i.e., does not engage in emotional incest); and 3) maintains an appropriate physical/sexual boundary (i.e., does not engage in physical incest).

Secondly, simple reparenting works for people whose primary problem is a simple deprivation neurosis. When this is compounded by other conditions, such as hysterical neurosis or character disorder, the process is far more complex and requires much caution and skill. See Baars & Terruwe, *op. cit.*

For an account of how the reparenting relationship can go wrong, see Conrad W. Baars, "When the Power to Heal Becomes Destructive," *Journal of Christian Healing*, 5.1 (Spring, 1983), 3–9. For a discussion of reparenting and an account of a successful reparenting relationship, see Gershen Kaufman, *op. cit.*, 119–159.

22. Kaufman writes, "Failure to fully hear and understand the other's need and to communicate its validity, whether or not we choose to gratify that need, breaks the interpersonal bridge and in so doing induces shame." *Op. cit.*, 14.

23. Baars, *Born Only Once, op. cit.*, 23.

24. St. Thomas Aquinas, *Summa Theologiae*, II-II, q. 161, a. 1, ad 3.

25. G.K. Chesterton, *Saint Thomas Aquinas* (Garden City, NY: Image, 1956), 119 and rest of Chapter IV, "A Meditation on the Manichees." See also Josef Pieper, *The Silence of Saint Thomas* (Chicago: Henry Regnery, 1957), especially Chapter II, "The Negative Element in the Philosophy of St. Thomas Aquinas."

26. Brian Swimme describes how even an ordinary activity like eating can be a way of remembering who we are and where we belong: "The physiological processes are the way the body remembers its ancestral heritage, and this heritage insists on particular natural foods for its remembering. . . . It is similar to what happens when you leaf through an old photo album. The pictures key all sorts of memories and you are flooded with the past coming alive within you. That's what eating is like. The foods enable patterns of activity to start up. If we understood that food was memory, we would stop our miserable eating habits." In

The Universe Is a Green Dragon: A Cosmic Creation Story (Santa Fe: Bear & Co., 1985), 105-106.

27. *Twelve Steps & Twelve Traditions, op. cit.*, 90. See also *Alcoholics Anonymous, op. cit.*, 66, 111, 116, 134.

28. H. Norman Wright, *Communication and Conflict Resolution in Marriage* (Elgin, IL: David C. Cooke, 1977), 6.

29. Weinhold, *Breaking Free of the Co-Dependency Trap, op. cit.*, has an excellent section on reparenting and how we can ask others for specific non-verbal ways we need nurturing. See pp. 194-208.

30. The capacity to consciously need other human beings and admit it was recognized by A.A. as essential for recovery long before we had a name for codependency: "*Need* is not, within Alcoholics Anonymous, a dirty word. The inability to say 'I need'—the *denial* of need—was what characterized the drinking alcoholic, who denied with special vehemence his very need for alcohol. A.A. began the restoration of the active alcoholic to sanity by enabling him to say 'I need.' Admitting the *need* for alcohol—and so implicitly for transcendence—was the First Step toward recovery. Accepting the need for others as the *real* route to transcendence was the rest of the A.A. program—and the foundation of the A.A. fellowship." In Kurtz. *op. cit.*, 218-219.

CHAPTER SIX: STEPS 4, 5, 6, AND 7
HEALING THE HURTS BENEATH WRONGS

1. Statistic is from *Newsweek*, July 8, 1991.

2. Bradshaw compares the symptoms of the wounded child with those of post-traumatic stress disorder. Cf. John Bradshaw, *Homecoming* (New York: Bantam, 1990), 216-217. Patrick Carnes makes the same comparison in *Don't Call It Love, op. cit.*, 125-130.

3. In his survey of recovering sex addicts (*Don't Call It*

Love, op cit., 195), Patrick Carnes found most slips and any decline in health occurred during the second half of the first year of sobriety when the addict was grieving the loss of his old life style. For the coaddict the first six months were the grief period and this was also the time of health decline and slips. The acting out of addictions became a way of avoiding the pain of grieving. Resolving grief heals addictive patterns and brings health. Note that the different time tables in grieving and recovery strain the marriage of an addict and coaddict unless each respects the other's unique journey. Recovering Couples Anonymous (RCA), PO Box 27617, Golden Valley, MN 55422 (612–473–3752) helps couples recover together.

4. Elisabeth Kübler-Ross, *On Death and Dying* (New York: Macmillan, 1969).

5. See Dennis & Matthew Linn, *Healing Life's Hurts: Healing Memories through the Five Stages of Forgiveness* (Mahwah, NJ: Paulist Press, 1978).

6. *Twelve Steps and Twelve Traditions, op. cit.*, 79-80.

7. *Ibid.*, 57–58.

8. *Alcoholics Anonymous, op. cit.*, 75.

CHAPTER SEVEN: STEPS 8 AND 9

1. Harold Kushner, *When All You've Ever Wanted Isn't Enough* (New York: Summit, 1986), 82.

2. Sandra Butler (ed.), *Conspiracy of Silence: The Trauma of Incest* (Denver: Kempe Nat. Ctr., 1978). For an excellent discussion of the dynamics of this "conspiracy," see Roland Summit, "Beyond Belief: The Reluctant Discovery of Incest." Summit argues that children cannot reveal sexual abuse because they become enmeshed in loyalty to adults, and because the adult world will neither listen to nor believe them: "The basic reason for disbelief is *adocentrism*, the unswerving and unquestioned allegiance to adult

values . . . *everyone* in the adult world finds some logical reason to defend the adult against the distress of the child." In Mary D. Pellauer, Barbara Chester & Jane Boyajian, *Sexual Assault and Abuse* (San Francisco: Harper & Row, 1987), 173.

3. An extensive study that is frequently cited found that 38% of women and 10% of men are physically sexually abused by the age of eighteen. Diane E. H. Russell, "The Incidence and Prevalence of Intrafamilial and Extrafamilial Sexual Abuse of Female Children," *Child Abuse and Neglect*, 7 (1983), 133–146. See also Mary D. Pellauer, et al., *op. cit.*, 13–14. Other studies indicate that the figures for men may be as high as those for women. Men, however, find it even harder to disclose experiences of abuse than women. Cf. Roland Summit, "Background, Identification and Evaluation of Child Sexual Abuse," *Childhelp USA Monograph*, 4 (June, 1983), 6. Alice Miller cites evidence that more than half of women in this country are sexually abused as children, and suggests that for every reported case there are at least fifty unreported cases. Cf. *Banished Knowledge* (New York: Doubleday, 1990), 60, 64–65.

4. Terry Kellogg, "From Codependency to Co-Creativity," talk delivered at the Conference of the Association of Christian Therapists, February, 1990.

5. Cf. Carnes, *Don't Call It Love, op. cit.*, 107ff.

6. See John Bradshaw, *Homecoming: Reclaiming and Championing Your Inner Child* (New York: Bantam, 1990), 41–43; Terry Kellogg, *Broken Toys Broken Dreams, op. cit.*, 272–273; Mellody, *Facing Codependence, op. cit.*, 162–169.

7. Mellody, *Facing Codependence, op. cit.*, 11–17.

8. Statistic for prostitutes reported by Ruth Norton, New Lifestyles Program (treatment program for prostitutes), St. Louis, Missouri, 1985. *Psychology Today* (May, 1984), 44.

9. Pellauer, et al., *op. cit.*, 176.

10. Carnes, *Don't Call It Love, op. cit.*, 146, 328–349.

11. "Any person who abuses his children has himself been

severely traumatized in his childhood in some form or another. This statement applies without exception since it is absolutely impossible for someone who has grown up in an environment of honesty, respect, and affection ever to feel driven to torment a weaker person in such a way as to inflict lifelong damage. He has learned very early on that it is right and proper to provide the small, helpless creature with protection and guidance; this knowledge, stored at that early stage in his mind and body, will remain effective for the rest of his life. . . . There is no reason for child abuse other than the repression of the abuse and confusion once suffered by the abuser himself." Miller, *op. cit.*, 190–191.

12. Reported at the 1987 convention of the American Orthopsychiatric Association in Washington, D.C.

13. "In order to develop relationships with boys, relationships which eventually are to include sexuality, a girl will first need to *practice* a bit on her dad. Likewise, the boy with his mother. This is what enables each child to then go out and build a complete relationship with a member of the opposite sex with confidence of satisfaction. Such practicing may take the form of flirtation, coquettishness, etc. What is needed is for the opposite sex parent simply to *accept* the boy's or girl's practicing and to *admire* his emerging masculinity or her emerging femininity . . . a girl needs both to identify with mother as well as have her femininity complemented by father who, in so doing, teaches her the joys of femininity . . . such 'complementarity' is a form of affirmation of the child's or adolescent's emerging manliness or womanliness." Kaufman, *op. cit.*, 63.

14. Mellody, *Permission to Be Precious, op. cit.*; Mellody, *Facing Codependence, op. cit.*, 150–153.

15. Mellody, *Facing Codependence, op. cit.*, 96–99. For a discussion of sexual abusers as shame-based, see Kaufman, *op. cit.*, 161–163 and Carnes, *Don't Call It Love, op. cit.*, 93–106. See also Alice Miller's entire book *Banished Knowledge, op. cit.*, for a profound exploration of the cycle of abuse.

In sexual abuse within the family (incest), the dynamics of self-blame are even more complex. The child cannot comprehend how a "good" parent would abuse a "good" child. Thus, the child is faced with two alternatives: either he or she is "bad" and thus deserving of abuse, or the parent is "bad" and thus capable of abusing an undeserving child. Since the child is utterly dependent on the parent for survival and even for solace in dealing with the pain of the abuse, the child finds it less terrifying to choose the former alternative. The child decides that he or she is the "bad" one and sets about trying to become "good" and thus deserving of better care. The result is not only self-blame, but also a split in the child's sense of reality: ". . . the bad has to be registered as good. This is a mind-splitting or a mind-fragmenting operation." Summit, quoting Leonard Shengold, in Pellauer, et al., *op. cit.*, 179.

16. *Twelve Steps & Twelve Traditions, op. cit.*, 90. See also *Alcoholics Anonymous, op. cit.*, 66, 111, 116, 134.

17. Miller, *op. cit.*, 167–175, 193-194.

18. *Ibid.*, 76.

19. Alice Miller describes how "forgiveness" can be used to manipulate and deny our feelings about how we have been abused, e.g., when a therapist tells a client, "Your hatred isn't good for you; it poisons your life and prolongs your dependence on your parents. Only when you become reconciled with your parents will you be free of them." Miller writes that, "Repressed, unconscious hatred has a destructive effect, whereas *relived* hatred is not a poison but one of the ways out of the trap of pretense, deceit or overt destructiveness. And the patient really does get well when he stops sparing the aggressors by harboring guilt feelings, when he finally dares to see and feel what they have done." *Ibid.*, 152–156.

20. For the relationship between shame and interpersonal bridges, see Kaufman, *op. cit.*, 11–24.

21. Miller, *op. cit.*, 13 & 170. See also 171, 192.

22. Terry Kellogg, "From Co-dependency to Co-creativity," *op. cit.*

23. In Japan not only alcoholics but also hardened prisoners are rehabilitated through Naikon Therapy, which has a prisoner record memories of being loved until he is spontaneously moved to make amends. Naikon Therapy is modeled on the Buddhist practice of reflecting alone each day from 5 AM to 9 PM. The therapist hears confessions revolving around three themes: what was received from others, what was returned to them and what troubles were caused to them. After days of reflection, the patient usually breaks down because he realizes how despite his selfishness others have loved him. The therapist then assigns the task of amending past wrongs so the future can be more positively lived. Dr. Stanton Samenow, author of *Inside the Criminal Mind*, uses a similar approach when treating psychopaths in the U.S. Cf. Dr. Ken Magid & Carole McKelvey, *High Risk: Children Without a Conscience* (New York: Bantam, 1988), 233–34.

24. Judith Viorst, *Necessary Losses* (New York: Fawcett, 1987), 32–33.

CHAPTER EIGHT: STEP 10

1. *Twelve Steps and Twelve Traditions*, *op. cit.*, 93.

2. *'Pass It On'*, *op. cit.*, 202.

3. See Kurtz, *op. cit.*, 95, 97, 183, 353, and *Twelve Steps and Twelve Traditions*, *op. cit.*, 55, 48–49.

4. Ann Belford Ulanov, *Receiving Woman* (Philadelphia: Westminster Press, 1981), 134. Based upon an essay by Valerie Saiving Goldstein, "The Human Situation: A Feminine Viewpoint," in Simon Doniger (ed.), *The Nature of Man in Theological and Psychological Perspective* (New York: Harper & Row, 1962), 151, 153, 165. Susan Dunfee makes a similar point when she identifies women's sin as not pride, meaning the attempt to

deny finitude, but rather as the "sin of hiding," meaning that women tend to deny their freedom, e.g., by living for others. She writes, "Until women repent of their real sin, the sin of having no self to sacrifice, they will know no end to the cycle of guilt and violence turned inward." Cf., Susan Nelson Dunfee, "The Sin of Hiding: A Feminist Critique of Reinhold Niebuhr's Account of the Sin of Pride," *Soundings*, Vol. 65, No. 3 (Fall, 1982), 324.

5. Charlotte Kasl, "The Twelve-Step Controversy," *Ms.* (November/ December, 1990), 31. For a more extensive discussion by Kasl of the special needs of women in recovery, see *Models of Recovery, op. cit.* (available from Charlotte Kasl, Box 7073, Minneapolis, MN 55407). See also her forthcoming book, *Many Roads, One Journey: Twelve-Step Programs in an Age of Diversity* (San Francisco: Harper & Row, 1992).

6. For a discussion of the addictive use of religion, see Peter Campbell, "Focusing: Doorway to the Body-Life of Spirit," *op. cit.*, 24, 26, 27, 50, 52. See also *Addictive Religion* and *"Process-Skipping,"* by Peter Campbell and Edwin McMahon, both available from Sheed & Ward, Kansas City, MO. Process-skipping is using something or someone to bypass listening to what is real inside. An example of process skipping with Jesus might be denying that we really feel angry and instead telling ourselves we *should* feel loving like Jesus. On religious addiction, see also Peter McCall, "Religious Addiction and Abuse," Dove Leaflet #32, available from Dove Publications, Pecos NM 87552. Religious addiction is intimately related to clericalism, which Michael Crosby defines as addiction to power and control. See his excellent and courageous book *The Dysfunctional Church* (Notre Dame: Ave Maria, 1991).

7. Anne Wilson Schaef, *Co-Dependence* (Minneapolis: Winston Press, 1986), 59.

8. Joseph Campbell with Bill Moyers, *The Power of Myth* (New York: Doubleday, 1988), 3.

9. *The Grapevine* (March, 1962), quoted in *As Bill Sees It*, *op. cit.*, 37.

CHAPTER NINE: STEP 11

1. Robert Thomsen, *Bill W.*, *op. cit.*, 189-190.
2. *Alcoholics Anonymous*, *op. cit.*, 10.
3. *'Pass It On'*, *op. cit.*, 124.
4. *Ibid.*, 120–121.
5. *Ibid.*, 121.
6. *Twelve Steps and Twelve Traditions*, *op. cit.*, 96–105.
7. *Alcoholics Anonymous*, *op. cit.*, 84–85.
8. *Twelve Steps and Twelve Traditions*, *op. cit.*, 34, 96. The phrase "*God as we understand God*" is underlined twice, once in Step 3 and once in Step 11.
9. The 12 Steps are principles for personal recovery. The 12 Traditions are principles for how 12 Step groups are to govern themselves and relate to the world.
10. *Twelve Steps and Twelve Traditions*, *op. cit.*, 132.
11. *Ibid.*, 140.
12. *Ibid.*, 139.
13. *Ibid.*, 172. See also *As Bill Sees It*, *op. cit.*, 98.
14. *Twelve Steps and Twelve Traditioins*, *op. cit.*, 143.
15. *Ibid.*, 142.
16. *'Pass It On'*, *op. cit.*, 125.
17. For how to do an intervention on someone who "shows no signs of wanting to reform," see Dr. Robert Stuckey, M.D., "You Gotta Have Hope," *New Catholic World*, Vol. 232, No. 1390 (July/August, 1989), 160–161.
18. *Twelve Steps and Twelve Traditions*, *op. cit.*, 136–138.
19. In other words, such passages are warnings intended to wake us up and deter us from destructive behavior. They are not

threats or predictions of what is inevitably going to happen to us. See John Sachs, "Current Eschatology: Universal Salvation and the Problem of Hell," *Theological Studies*, 52 (1991), 238.

20. Dick Westley, *Redemptive Intimacy: A New Perspective for the Journey to Adult Faith* (Mystic, CT: Twenty-Third, 1981), 111–112.

21. For how Anselmian salvation theology represents only one of the three dominant New Testament theologies, see Dick Westley, *op. cit.*, 112ff. In the twelfth century Abelard took a different point of view than had Anselm, described as follows by Joseph Campbell, "Jesus' death on the cross was not as ransom paid, or as a penalty applied, but an act of atonement, at-one-ment, with the race." By becoming "at one" with the suffering of life, Jesus evokes the human sentiment of compassion. His cross invites us to focus our hearts on compassionately living for one another. Cf. Campbell, *The Power of Myth, op. cit.*, 112.

22. Raymond E. Brown, *The Gospels and Epistles of John* (Collegeville: Liturgical Press, 1988), 80. In classical Greek, long before the New Testament writings appeared, the word "para-kletos" was used in a legal sense to refer to a defense attorney.

23. Jesus' solidarity with sinners includes the chained demons mentioned in the Book of Enoch and those in Noah's time who were punished by the flood because they "refused to believe." Jesus chooses to die as one of them, a sinner, abandoned by God and crying out in Mk. 15:32, "My God, my God, why have you abandoned me?" Thus, Jesus, as God's own son, "experiences the 'hell' of the Father's absence in a way impossible for any other person." Sachs, *op. cit.*, 244 and *The Jerusalem Bible* (Garden City: Doubleday, 1966), 495, footnote h.

24. Hans Urs von Balthasar, translated excerpt from "Abstieg zur Hölle," quoted in *The Von Balthasar Reader*, Medard Kehl & Werner Loser (eds.) (New York: Crossroad, 1982), 153. Cited in Sachs, *op. cit.*, 244.

25. *Twelve Steps and Twelve Traditions, op. cit.*, 140.

26. *Ibid.*, 141.

27. Sachs, *op. cit.*, 237–239.

28. Sachs, *ibid.*, 242.

29. Sachs, *ibid.*, 247.

30. Carl Rogers, *On Becoming a Person* (Boston: Houghton Mifflin, 1961), 101–103.

31. Andrew Greeley, *The Religious Imagination* (New York: William Sadlier, 1981), 211.

32. Quoted in Sachs, *op. cit.*, 254.

33. Stuckey, *op. cit.*, 161–162.

34. Bill W. spoke of those who hurt us as "spiritually sick," and urged the same compassionate attitude toward them as we would have toward a sick friend. *As Bill Sees It, op. cit.*, 286.

35. *As Bill Sees It, op. cit.*, 98.

CHAPTER TEN: STEP 12

1. For more on Erikson's eight stages of human development, see our book, *Healing the Eight Stages of Life*, (Mahwah, NJ: Paulist, 1988).

2. *Grapevine* (January, 1958).

3. *Alcoholics Anonymous, op. cit.*, 94. Bill applied this advice to other problems as well. For example, when troubled by sexual temptations, one should focus on the needs of others and try harder to help them. *Ibid.*, 70.

4. *'Pass It On', op. cit.*, 335.

5. Melody Beattie, *Codependent No More* (New York: Harper, 1987), 79.

6. These questions come from reflecting on the rescue triangle developed by Stephen Karpman. Cf., Claude Steiner, *Scripts People Live* (New York: Grove Press, 1974).

7. Kurtz, *op. cit.*, 38–39.

8. Bill Moyers' PBS interview with Dr. T. Berry Brazelton, in Bill Moyers, A *World of Ideas* (New York: Doubleday, 1989), 140–155.

9. Rep. Joe Moakley, Chairman of the Speaker's Special Task Force on El Salvador, has gathered evidence for the interpretation of events presented here. Cf. *National Catholic Reporter* (October 4, 1991), 8.

10. Joanna Rogers Macy, *Despair and Personal Power in the Nuclear Age* (Philadelphia: New Society Pub., 1983).

11. Thomsen, *op. cit.*, 310.

12. *Twelve Steps and Twelve Traditions, op. cit.*, 121.

13. Campbell, *The Power of Myth, op. cit.*, 120.

14. Robert A. Johnson, *Ecstasy: Understanding the Psychology of Joy* (San Francisco: Harper & Row, 1987).

APPENDIX A: USING THE IMAGINATION FOR HEALING AND RECOVERY

1. *Twelve Steps and Twelve Traditions, op. cit.*, 100.

2. Mark Mitchell, MFCC, *Sober Times* (July, 1988), San Diego; also cited in Yoder, *op. cit.*, 65.

3. Bernard Siegel, *Love, Medicine and Miracles* (New York: Harper & Row, 1986).

4. Mark J. Mitchell, MFCC, *op. cit.*; also cited in Yoder, *op. cit.*, 65.

5. Patrick Carnes, *Don't Call It Love, op. cit.*, 290–91.

6. *Twelve Steps and Twelve Traditions, op. cit.*, 106–07.

About the Authors

DENNIS, SHEILA AND MATT LINN work together as a team, integrating physical, emotional and spiritual wholeness through their work as hospital chaplains, therapists and retreat directors. As a team they have taught courses on healing in over thirty countries and in many universities, including a course for doctors accredited by the American Medical Association. Matt and Dennis are the authors of ten books, including *Healing of Memories, Healing Life's Hurts, Deliverance Prayer, Healing the Dying* (with Sr. Mary Jane Linn) and *To Heal as Jesus Healed* (with Barbara Shlemon). Sheila, Dennis and Matt together have written *Prayer Course for Healing Life's Hurts, Praying with Another for Healing, Healing the Greatest Hurt* and *Healing the Eight Stages of Life*. These books have sold over a million copies in English and have been translated into eleven different languages.